# Brief Dynamic
# Therapy

# Theories of Psychotherapy Series

**Theories of Psychotherapy Series**
Jon Carlson and Matt Englar-Carlson, Series Editors

# Brief Dynamic Therapy

Hanna Levenson

American Psychological Association

Washington, DC

First Printing February 2010
Second Printing December 2010
Third Printing August 2015

Published by
American Psychological Association
750 First Street, NE
Washington, DC 20002
www.apa.org

To order
APA Order Department
P.O. Box 92984
Washington, DC 20090-2984
Tel: (800) 374-2721;
Direct: (202) 336-5510
Fax: (202) 336-5502;
TDD/TTY: (202) 336-6123
Online: www.apa.org/books/
E-mail: order@apa.org

In the U.K., Europe, Africa, and the Middle East, copies may be ordered from
American Psychological Association
3 Henrietta Street
Covent Garden, London
WC2E 8LU England

Typeset in Minion by Shepherd Inc., Dubuque, IA

Printer: United Book Press, Inc., Baltimore, MD
Cover Designer: Minker Design, Sarasota, FL
Cover Art: *Lily Rising*, 2005, oil and mixed media on panel in craquelure frame, by Betsy Bauer.

The opinions and statements published are the responsibility of the authors, and such opinions and statements do not necessarily represent the policies of the American Psychological Association.

**Library of Congress Cataloging-in-Publication Data**

Levenson, Hanna, 1945-
  Brief dynamic therapy / Hanna Levenson. -- 1st ed.
      p. ; cm. -- (APA theories of psychotherapy series)
  Includes bibliographical references and index.
  ISBN-13: 978-1-4338-0755-8
  ISBN-10: 1-4338-0755-6
  1. Brief psychotherapy. 2. Psychodynamic psychotherapy. I. American Psychological Association. II. Title. III. Series: APA theories of psychotherapy series.
  [DNLM: 1. Psychotherapy, Brief. 2. Psychological Theory. WM 420.5.P5 L657b 2010]
  RC480.55.L477 2010
  616.89'14--dc22
                                        2009041272

British Library Cataloguing-in-Publication Data
A CIP record is available from the British Library.

*Printed in the United States of America*
*First Edition*

To my clients and students—with gratitude for relationships
filled with meaning and feeling

# Contents

# Series Preface

Some might argue that in the contemporary clinical practice of psychotherapy, evidence-based intervention and effective outcome have overshadowed theory in importance. Maybe. But, as the editors of this series, we don't propose to take up that controversy here. We do know that psychotherapists adopt and practice according to one theory or another because their experience, and decades of good evidence, suggests that having a sound theory of psychotherapy leads to greater therapeutic success. Still, the role of theory in the helping process can be hard to explain. This narrative about solving problems helps convey theory's importance:

> Aesop tells the fable of the sun and wind having a contest to decide who was the most powerful. From above the earth, they spotted a man walking down the street, and the wind said that he bet he could get his coat off. The sun agreed to the contest. The wind blew and the man held on tightly to his coat. The more the wind blew, the tighter he held. The sun said it was his turn. He put all of his energy into creating warm sunshine and soon the man took off his coat.

What does a competition between the sun and the wind to remove a man's coat have to do with theories of psychotherapy? We think this deceptively simple story highlights the importance of theory as the precursor to any effective intervention—and hence to a favorable outcome. Without a guiding theory, we might treat the symptom without understanding the role of the individual. Or we might create power conflicts with our clients and not understand that, at times, indirect means of helping (sunshine) are often as effective—if not more so—than direct ones (wind). In the absence of theory, we might lose track of the treatment rationale and instead get caught up in, for example, social correctness and not wanting to do something that looks too simple.

What exactly *is* theory? The *APA Dictionary of Psychology* defines theory as "a principle or body of interrelated principles that purports to explain or predict a number of interrelated phenomena." In psychotherapy, a theory is a set of principles used to explain human thought and behavior, including what causes people to change. In practice, a theory creates the goals of therapy and specifies how to pursue them. Haley (1997) noted that a theory of psychotherapy ought to be simple enough for the average therapist to understand, but comprehensive enough to account for a wide range of eventualities. Furthermore, a theory guides action toward successful outcomes while generating hope in both the therapist and client that recovery is possible.

Theory is the compass that allows psychotherapists to navigate the vast territory of clinical practice. In the same ways that navigational tools have been modified to adapt to advances in thinking and ever-expanding territories to explore, theories of psychotherapy have changed over time. The different schools of theories are commonly referred to as waves, the first wave being psychodynamic theories (i.e., Adlerian, psychoanalytic), the second wave learning theories (i.e., behavioral, cognitive–behavioral), the third wave humanistic theories (person-centered, gestalt, existential), the fourth wave feminist and multicultural theories, and the fifth wave postmodern and constructivist theories. In many ways, these waves represent how psychotherapy has adapted and responded to changes in psychology, society, and epistemology as well as to changes in the nature of psychotherapy itself. Psychotherapy and the theories that guide it are dynamic and responsive. The wide variety of theories is also testament to the different ways in which the same human behavior can be conceptualized (Frew & Spiegler, 2008).

It is with these two concepts in mind—the central importance of theory and the natural evolution of theoretical thinking—that we developed the APA Theories of Psychotherapy Series. Both of us are thoroughly fascinated by theory and the range of complex ideas that drive each model. As university faculty members who teach courses on the theories of psychotherapy, we wanted to create learning materials that not only highlight the essence of the major theories for professionals and professionals in training but also clearly bring the reader up to date on the current status of the models. Often in books on theory, the biography of the original theorist overshadows the evolution of the model. In contrast, our intent is to highlight the contemporary uses of the theories as well as their history and context.

As this project began, we faced two immediate decisions: which theories to address and who best to present them. We looked at graduate-level theories of psychotherapy courses to see which theories are being taught, and we explored popular scholarly books, articles, and conferences to determine which theories draw the most interest. We then developed a dream list of authors from among the best minds in contemporary theoretical practice. Each author is one of the leading proponents of that approach as well as a knowledgeable practitioner. We asked each author to review the core constructs of the theory, bring the theory into the modern sphere of clinical practice by looking at it through a context of evidence-based practice, and clearly illustrate how the theory looks in action.

There are 24 titles planned for the series. Each title can stand alone or can be put together with a few other titles to create materials for a course in psychotherapy theories. This option allows instructors to create a course featuring the approaches they believe are the most salient today. To support this end, APA Books has also developed a DVD for each of the approaches that demonstrates the theory in practice with a real client. Many of the DVDs show therapy over six sessions. Contact APA Books for a complete list of available DVD programs (http://www.apa.org/videos).

A common assumption about psychodynamic psychotherapy is that it is a model best suited for long-term clients, yet the marketplace for psychotherapy has increasingly moved toward short-term therapy. In *Brief Dynamic Therapy,* Dr. Hanna Levenson outlines a model of psychodynamic practice that fits the reality of short-term therapy, called time-limited dynamic psychotherapy. Dr. Levenson places this approach in the context of other brief forms of psychotherapy and shows how significant change can occur in a short amount of time. Dr. Levenson explains this integrative, empathic approach by using clinical illustrations and drawing from research studies on the efficacy of brief therapy. Readers will learn much from this pragmatic book, which offers clear steps for effective short-term psychodynamic clinical work that is brief, focused, and deep.

—Jon Carlson and Matt Englar-Carlson

## REFERENCES

Frew, J., & Spiegler, M. (2008). *Contemporary psychotherapies for a diverse world.* Boston, MA: Lahaska Press.

Haley, J. (1997). *Leaving home: The therapy of disturbed young people.* New York, NY: Routledge.

# Brief Dynamic
# Therapy

# 1

# Introduction

## WHAT IS BRIEF THERAPY?

To set the stage for defining brief therapy, I'd like to tell the story of what happened when I began one of my first real jobs in clinical psychology some 30 years ago. I was hired by a VA Medical Center (VAMC) to start a program to train third-year psychiatry residents and psychology predoctoral interns how to do brief therapy. At the time, the outpatient psychiatry department was being flooded with Vietnam veterans seeking help. The clinicians, who were used to seeing their clients for extended periods of time (sometimes decades), were getting burned out. More and more patients were being added to their rosters, but no one was terminating. In my employment interview with the then Director of the Outpatient Service, he let it be known that while it seemed briefer forms of intervention might be warranted, they "would never work at the VA because the veterans thought of the VA as home." Not an auspicious way to start a new position!

The model of training I used back then involved a fixed upper limit of 20 sessions—not for some totally theoretical reason, but mainly because the trainees' rotation at the site was 6 months long. I figured that within that amount of time, trainees and clients would have approximately

3

20 weeks available in which to do therapy. The training was designed to mirror the time-limited nature of the therapy; we met concurrently for a 3-hour seminar/consultation weekly for 21 weeks.

I stayed at the VA for 20 years, heading up what came to be known as the VA Brief Therapy Program. During that time several hundred trainees and (some staff) completed the program. When I retired from the VA, I was still using the same 20-session model. However, the length of most of the treatments provided by my colleagues located in other VA psychiatry inpatient and outpatient services had become increasing shorter and shorter for the same financial ("cost-effective") reasons that caused therapies to become briefer in the private sector. As time went on, my colleagues would often make referrals of complex cases to the Brief Therapy Program knowing that those clients would be seen for a longer period of time in my "brief" program than elsewhere. The moral of the story is that often what is considered brief is, to some extent, *in the eyes of the beholder* (and reflected in the zeitgeist).

To further underscore the point, I remember one of my first brief therapy cases when I was an intern at a training site with a reputation for psychoanalytically oriented, long-term therapy. After a couple of sessions, I needed to tell the client that I would only be able to see her for 3 months. I practiced saying it over and over so that my voice would not betray the guilt I felt in not giving her "enough." When I finally worked up the courage to tell her, she exclaimed, "Is it really going to take that long?"

## EVERYONE DOES BRIEF THERAPY

If you are a practicing therapist or studying to be one, I know you are probably doing brief therapy. In a national survey of almost 4,000 mental health professionals, Levenson and Davidovitz (2000) found that almost 90% of psychologists do some form of therapy that is *designed to be time limited* and focused, and psychodynamically oriented therapists conduct one quarter of all the planned brief therapy in the United States.[1] In addi-

---

[1] This does not mean, however, that these therapists felt competent to do brief therapy. In fact, Levenson and Davidovitz (2000) found that half of the psychologists doing therapies that were planned to be brief *never* had any course work in the subject. And those psychodynamic therapists who were doing short-term work were less skilled and trained in it than their colleagues from other orientations.

tion, everyone does *unplanned brief therapies* because most clients choose to stay in therapy a brief amount of time, whether or not the therapist has other ideas. For example, Olfson and Pincus (1994) found that 70% of outpatients in the United States were seen for 10 or fewer sessions. Over the years, it has been well documented that most people who enter therapy (even those treatments that are designed to be long term and open-ended) drop out by the eighth session (Phillips, 1985; Rau, 1989; Wierzbicki & Pekarik, 1993), with a median treatment length of approximately six sessions (Garfield, 1994). As remarked by Muran and colleagues (2009), "these high dropout rates are comparable to those found over 50 years ago" (p. 234). Budman and Gurman (1988) have termed these "premature terminations" as *brief therapies by default* (as compared to *brief therapies by design*). We tend to forget that long before third-party payers began setting limits on treatment, clients themselves did.[2]

Most people who are coming for therapy are in emotional pain, and they want to have this pain alleviated as soon as possible. They are not fascinated by their psyches, nor do they seek mental health perfectionism. Sometimes clients experience their needs for immediate relief at variance with their therapists' goals for "problem resolution." Oftentimes, too, clients feel adrift in open-ended therapies where they do know what the goals are or how the process will benefit them. "Where are we going?" "What are we doing?" "Am I making progress?" are frequently asked questions.

Having said this, I need to make an important point with regard to *how brief* brief therapy can be. "Since the advent of psychotherapy, one of the most common questions has been, 'how much psychotherapy is enough'" (Cameron, 2006). When we speak of brief dynamic psychotherapy today, the usual time frame is considered to be anywhere from 8 to 25 sessions (Koss & Shiang, 1994; Shapiro et al., 1994). This must be distinguished from what has been called *ultra brief therapy* or managed care therapy. In examining a national database of more than 6,000 patients, Hansen,

---

[2] In a recent article, Swift, Callahan, and Levine (2009) discuss theoretical issues and empirical findings regarding the definition of "premature termination." For example, who is considered a "dropout" may be based on not completing a specified number of sessions, therapist judgment, or leaving therapy before one has attained clinical improvement. These authors found a dropout rate of 77% when they used the criterion of clients' discontinuing treatment before achieving clinically significant change.

Lambert, and Forman (2002) found that the average number of sessions patients received through managed care organizations or employee assistance programs was less than five! As stated by Levenson and Burg (2000) in their discussion of training psychologists in the era of managed care, the empirical basis of such ultra brief therapies is minimal or unsupported. Therefore, the reader should keep in mind that when I am talking about brief dynamic therapy, I am referring to therapy that relies on the development of a meaningful therapeutic relationship.[3] But brief dynamic therapy is about so much more than just limited time. It is not condensed long-term therapy nor what you do when you can't do "real" (i.e., long-term) therapy. The following section explicates the parameters that are core to brief dynamic therapies.

## QUALITIES THAT DEFINE BRIEF DYNAMIC PSYCHOTHERAPY

When we talk about brief dynamic psychotherapy, to what are we referring? Are there essential characteristics that brief dynamic psychotherapies have in common and that also distinguish them from more open-ended or longer-term models? A number of years ago, I (Levenson & Butler, 1994) did a content analysis of as many publications as I could find addressing this topic. After doing an up-to-date review of more recent articles, chapters, and books on the topic for this book, I found the same fundamental qualities discovered previously. Some of these qualities are mentioned repeatedly in the literature and, therefore, appear to be quite essential in defining brief dynamic psychotherapy; others are less frequently reported and seem more peripheral.[4] These characteristics may be conceptualized as a consensual, operational definition of short-term dynamic psychotherapy and will be listed below in two main categories: those qualities pertaining to the *brief features* per se and those germane to the *psychodynamic aspects*.

---

[3] Although there is literature on brief dynamic therapy as applied to groups and couples, my focus in this book will be chiefly on individual psychotherapy.

[4] One author (Binder, 2004), however, has challenged whether these qualities are unique to time-limited approaches, arguing that they are characteristic of good psychotherapy in general regardless of length. While I am basically in agreement with Binder that a well-delivered brief dynamic psychotherapy is basically good, sound therapy, it is helpful to observe that brief dynamic approaches are likely to delineate more limited treatment foci and more specific goals than their longer-term counterparts.

## Modifications to Make Therapy Briefer

### *Limited Therapeutic Focus and Goals*

The chief factor distinguishing brief from long-term dynamic psychotherapy is its circumscribed focus. Even before mentioning the concept of time, writers agree that "articulating a clinical focus or foci is a hallmark characteristic of all brief psychotherapy approaches" (Messer & Warren, 1995, p. 126). Therapists need a central theme, topic, or problem to guide the work when time is limited. Yogi Berra, former catcher for the New York Yankees known for his idiosyncratic use of the English language, captured the essence of this quality, "If you don't know where you're going, you will wind up somewhere else."

As Joseph Weiss (1993) wrote definitively in his book on how psychotherapy works,

> When I was a student at the San Francisco Psychoanalytic Institute, a prominent teacher advised me to avoid formulating the patient's problems, especially at the beginning of treatment. He assumed that in general it is possible to formulate a case only after a prolonged period of exploration, and so that if the therapist develops hypotheses about the patient too early, he risks the premature closure of his mind. *I now believe that this advice is wrong.* (emphasis added, p. 70)

Binder (2004), in his excellent book outlining the competencies of the brief dynamic psychotherapist, perceptively delineates two different therapeutic skills having to do with focusing. The first is the ability to discern what will constitute the focus of the work, and the second is how to track and maintain this focus throughout the therapy.

Related to, but distinct from, therapeutic focus is the concept of limited goals. The aim of brief dynamic psychotherapy is not "cure" once and for all. Rather, the therapy should provide an opportunity to foster some changes in behavior, thinking, and feeling, permitting more adaptive coping, improved interpersonal relationships, and a better sense of one's self. Brief dynamic therapy is seen as an opportunity to begin a process of change that (hopefully) continues long after the therapy is over. Clearly both therapist *and* client need to accept limits.

## Time Limits and Time Management

Naturally, the amount of time is the obvious variable that defines an approach as *short-term, brief,* or *time-limited.* The issue of time is the second most frequently mentioned brief therapy criterion. Most modern brief dynamic clinicians set 20–25 sessions as the upper limit of brief therapy (Koss & Shiang, 1994; Levenson, 1995; Preston, Varzos, & Liebert, 1995). Usually the *limiting* or *rationing* of time is used conceptually to accelerate the therapeutic work, either by raising the patient's awareness of the existential issues of finite time and mortality (e.g., Mann, 1973) or by encouraging therapist activity and adherence to a focus (e.g., Horowitz et al., 1984).

Although it is most customary for psychodynamically oriented short-term therapists to use the traditional weekly 50-minute "hour," many experiment with the frequency, duration, and number of sessions. Brief dynamic therapists have felt that limiting the length of the therapy encourages individuation, autonomy, and positive expectations. Also there is some intriguing evidence that providing time limits actually might encourage those clients who otherwise might terminate "prematurely" in an open-ended format to stay in therapy longer (Hilsenroth, Ackerman, & Blagys, 2001; Sledge, Moras, Hartley, & Levine, 1990).

Recently, brief dynamic therapists are moving away from conceptualizing therapy merely in terms of a specific amount of time and are instead addressing ways to make every session count regardless of length of treatment. These models are categorized as *time-attentive* or *time-efficient,* where the notion of "brevity" is more an attitude in the therapist's mind that affects the work. Also, brief therapists are comfortable with the idea of rendering help for short periods throughout the client's life cycle (Budman & Gurman, 1988; Cummings, 1995). For example, I have been in practice long enough (30 years) that I have seen some clients for three or four different brief therapies at various stages in their lives.

Unfortunately, with today's economic belt-tightening, time limits have been used increasingly for administrative and monetary reasons instead of therapeutic ones. In the worst of situations, there may be no therapeutic rationale for the number of sessions clients receive—such decisions being driven solely by the financial bottom line (Levenson & Burg, 2000).

### Selection Criteria

The importance of selection criteria is a controversial subject in the brief dynamic psychotherapy field. Early in the history of psychoanalysis, as psychoanalytic treatments became progressively longer, Freud (1904/1953) put forth the possibility that treatment might be shortened, but only for psychologically healthier patients. Thus, early practitioners of brief dynamic therapy emphasized rigorous patient selection (choosing those who were psychologically minded, highly motivated, and of above average intelligence, for example). Current short-term therapists tend to take a more process orientation and judge if lengthening the therapy is warranted as the work progresses.

### Therapist Activity

Brief dynamic psychotherapy requires the therapist to be an active participant in the process. However, *activity* is only needed to the extent necessary to maintain the *focus*, foster a *positive alliance*, and make progress within a certain amount of *time*. Thus, activity is integrally related to the aforementioned aspects of focus and time. Many clinicians, when learning brief therapy techniques, become confused that therapist activity means confrontation, advice giving, and/or outright direction. What it more appropriately entails is an awareness of the goals of the work and a plan of how to get there, while being sensitive to the client's presentation and the context of the clinical material. Thus, therapist activity can range from *supportive interventions* (e.g., reassurance, strengthening of adaptive defenses) to more *exploratory* ones (e.g., interpretation, confrontation) depending upon factors (e.g., strength of the therapeutic alliance) emerging in the session as well as client characteristics (e.g., psychological health, quality of interpersonal relationships).

### Therapeutic Alliance

The strength of the therapeutic alliance, especially from the client's perspective, has long been shown to be one of the major factors predicting outcome (Horvarth & Greenberg, 1994; Martin, Garske, & Davis, 2000; Orlinsky, Grawe, & Parks, 1994). Although various researchers define the alliance somewhat differently, it is generally thought of as comprised of the emotional bond between therapist and client, and an agreement on the goals and means to accomplish those goals. The quality of the alliance early in therapy has been shown to predict client dropout and the amount of "work" done in sessions (e.g., Piper et al., 1999). Thus, while forming a positive alliance as quickly as possible is important in all therapies, it is of critical importance in brief therapy where the therapist might not get many opportunities to repair ruptures in the therapeutic relationship.

### Rapid Assessment/Prompt Intervention

The therapist's ability to formulate the client's case and begin intervening quickly is also imperative. When I was an intern at the aforementioned setting famous for its psychoanalytic training program, we spent approximately 3 months getting a full history and developing an understanding of the client's dynamics *prior* to accepting the client for treatment. Today those 3 months could constitute the total time frame allotted for an entire therapy.

### Termination

The brief therapist must be willing to terminate with clients in a considered manner. Because the therapy is short term, termination is woven into the fabric of the work from the beginning. If the ending of a brief dynamic therapy is handled poorly, previously good therapeutic work can be undone. Training in this final phase of treatment is of the utmost importance. However, it has been my experience that many trainees (even those almost finished with their professional education) have never seen the beginning, middle, and *planned ending* of one case!

### Optimism

In their book on *Models of Brief Psychodynamic Therapy*, Messer and Warren (1995) consider how the psychoanalytic vision of human reality is more "tragic" (with people seen as trapped and suffering), while briefer approaches are characterized by a more "comic" outlook. "The brief therapist approaches therapy in a more optimistic spirit, believing that worthwhile change is achievable within the set time limit" (p. 42).

My colleagues and I have compared the attitudes of short-term to long-term therapists (Bolter, Levenson, & Alvarez, 1990) and found that the brief practitioners are more likely to believe that psychological change occurs outside of therapy and that setting time limits intensifies the therapeutic work. In another study, Levenson and Bolter (1988) examined the values and attitudes of psychiatry residents and psychology interns before and after a 6-month training in time-limited dynamic psychotherapy and found that, post-training, students were more willing to consider using brief therapy, more positive about achieving significant insight, more expectant that the benefits would be long lasting, and less likely to think that extensive "working through" is necessary. Also, they were more willing to be active and to believe that clients would continue to change after the therapy was over. Similarly, experienced therapists became more positive and optimistic toward brief therapy following a daylong workshop on the topic (Neff et al., 1997).

### Contract

The final major difference between shorter-term versus longer-term dynamic therapies concerns setting up a therapeutic contract. This contract is "neither legalistic nor necessarily written" (Hobbs, 2006, p. 120). The degree of specificity of such a contract varies, but at the very least there is an understanding at the outset of the therapy that the work will be limited in time and/or focused in scope. Some brief models, like those of Mann's (1973) time-limited therapy, are designed to motivate clients by giving a precise contract of 12 sessions; others are more abstract, telling the client that they will work on a certain area of concern that could take about 3 to 6 months.

## Modifications of Psychoanalytic Concepts and Techniques

Brief dynamic therapy relies on major psychoanalytic and psychodynamic concepts such as the importance of childhood experiences and developmental history, unconscious (or out-of-awareness) determinants of behavior, the role of conflict, transference-countertransference phenomena, the therapeutic alliance, and repetitive behavior. However, postmodern, brief dynamic therapists eschew highly inferential psychoanalytic concepts (e.g., Oedipus complex, psychosexual stages of development).

Also the brief dynamic therapist is more likely to emphasize the client's *strengths* and resources in dealing with real-life issues, rather than fostering regression and fantasy. Therefore, such psychoanalytic methods, such as free association or lying on the couch, are not used. Another major modification of psychoanalytic technique is that there is more emphasis on the here-and-now of the client's life than the there-and-then of childhood. For many modern brief therapists, interpretation (especially transference interpretation) plays a less central role, and insight, while still important, is not considered *the* panacea.[5]

Not only are traditional psychoanalytic interventions modified, but techniques from other theoretical approaches such as experiential–process therapy and cognitive–behavioral therapy may be incorporated (Fosha, 2000; Levenson, 1995; Magnavita, 1997; McCullogh Vaillant, 1997; Safran & Muran, 2000). In brief dynamic treatments, the understanding of clients in terms of psychodynamic theory is decoupled from the exclusive use of dynamic techniques. The brief dynamic therapist may be thinking psychodynamically but feels free to use a variety of intervention strategies. The next chapter will present these (and other) modifications in an historical context.

## SUMMARY AND INTENT

In summary, short-term psychodynamic psychotherapies can be described as treatments of limited duration in which therapists are active in maintaining a circumscribed focus with limited goals while using a framework of basic, psychodynamically derived concepts with wide-ranging techniques.

While I have presented some general characteristics that distinguish short-term from long-term orientations, there is no single approach called "brief dynamic psychotherapy." As will become obvious in the following chapters, there is quite an array of approaches that all fit within this rubric. In an effort to make brief dynamic therapy concepts come alive for the reader, I refer to a particular brief dynamic therapy—time-limited dynamic psychotherapy (TLDP)—throughout the text to illustrate ways of formulating and intervening in a timely manner. It is my intention to use TLDP as a vehicle for introducing the reader to the applicability

---

[5] However, the definition of what constitutes "insight" is quite complex. The reader is referred to a book edited by Louis Castonguay and Clara Hill (2007) on insight in psychotherapy for more information.

of brief dynamic approaches for today's practicing clinician. TLDP is a model with which I am quite familiar from clinical (Levenson, 1995, 2003; Levenson & Strupp, 2007), training (Levenson & Burg, 2000; Levenson & Evans, 2000; Levenson & Strupp, 1999), and empirical (Levenson & Bein, 1993; Levenson & Overstreet, 1993) perspectives. It is an *integrative* short-term approach that interweaves major principles of time-sensitive clinical work. I hope it will capture the breadth and depth of what brief dynamic psychotherapy can offer.

# History

As it is said, the history of short-term dynamic therapy is long. From a historical and conceptual viewpoint, brief dynamic psychotherapies may be conveniently grouped into "generations" (Crits-Christoph, Barber, & Kurcias, 1991). As with all generations, customary ways of doing things are passed down, embraced, and become beloved or unquestioned traditions, and then are challenged and replaced by the "younger generation of whippersnappers." I will delineate four such generations as a way of tracing the evolution in the thinking and practice of brief dynamic psychotherapy.[1] The history of these four generations can also be described, as Fosha (1995) so ingeniously puts it, as "a story of progressive taboo breaking; [where] with each step, a different psychoanalytic taboo must be confronted and broken" (p. 297). *—> Love that!*

---

[1] For further information on the early history of brief dynamic psychotherapy, the reader is referred to overviews by Marmor (1979), Messer and Warren (1995), Crits-Cristoph and Barber (1991), and Bauer and Kobos (1987) as well as to the original works.

## FIRST GENERATION: FREUD AND HIS FOLLOWERS AND PSYCHOANALYSIS

Contemporary brief dynamic psychotherapy is anchored in the work of Freud. In fact, Bauer and Kobos (1987) unequivocally state that "[b]rief psychotherapy was born when Freud renounced hypnosis as an effective treatment technique" (p. 13). Several of Freud's early treatments were short-term therapies. Bruno Walter, the famous conductor, wrote in his autobiography that he was treated successfully by Freud in 1906 for partial paralysis of his right arm in six sessions (Walter, 1940). Reportedly, Freud prescribed a vacation for Walter following which he was to return to his conducting (Sterba, 1951). When Walter protested fearing embarrassment should he not be able to conduct while on stage, Freud said he would accept complete responsibility! And in 1908 Freud purportedly cured the composer Gustav Mahler of impotency problems in a single-session therapy during a four-hour walk in a Viennese park (Flegenheimer, 1982; Jones, 1955)—giving new meaning to the colloquial expression, "It was a walk in the park!" Even training analyses were conducted in less than one year. During this time, Freud, the brief therapist, used suggestion, catharsis, and education to accomplish the chief goal of psychoanalysis—to make conscious what is unconscious (Freud, 1933).

However, as Freud became less fond of these active interventions, he adopted a more passive stance, and the therapies became less focused. As a consequence, the therapies became longer. Psychoanalytic theory became more complex and elaborate, and the goals of analysis became more ambitious. These too increased treatment length. When Freud made the switch from catharsis to a growing reliance on free association, it was, as Davanloo (1986) noted, a "fateful step."

> Almost all attempts to reverse this trend and develop an effective technique of short-term psychotherapy have been based on taking back some of the control and putting more of the motive power [for the treatment] into the hands of the therapist. (p. 108)

Similarly, Malan (1980) observed:

> It needs to be stated categorically that in the early part of this century Freud unwittingly took a wrong turn which led to disastrous

consequences for the future of psychotherapy. This was to react to increasing resistance with increased passivity—eventually adopting the technique of free association on the part of the patient, and the role of "passive sounding board," free-floating attention, and infinite patience on the part of the therapist. (p. 13)

By the time of his death, however, Freud was quite disillusioned with the effectiveness of these "interminable" analyses and concluded that it "was a lengthy business" (Freud, 1937) with sometimes disappointing results.

Fosha (1995) credits psychoanalysis with breaking the taboo prohibiting everything but polite social discourse. Freud delved into the nether regions of the unconsciousness mind, exploring sexual and aggressive impulses and fantasies, and the world has not been the same since. Grotjahn (1966) put it quite poetically, "It might be said that Sigmund Freud disturbed the sleep of the world" (p. 47).

I would like to apply Fosha's concept of taboo breaking to other brief therapy pioneers and practitioners.[2] In this way, hopefully, it will become clear how these innovators were dedicated to (re)discovering and devising strategies and techniques that would more efficiently and effectively lessen their patients' suffering, even if it meant going against prescribed, established psychoanalytic principles ("the pure gold of analysis").

Sandor Ferenczi (1920/1950) challenged many psychoanalytic taboos. First and foremost, he criticized the passive therapist stance. A contemporary of Freud's, he saw that "psychoanalysis as we employ it today, is a procedure whose most prominent characteristic is passivity" (p. 199). He believed that the technique of interpretation was not a powerful enough change agent and saw that the therapist had to be more direct. Not only did he encourage activities previously avoided by the patient, he also prohibited certain behaviors (e.g., rituals). Ferenczi compared his "active therapy" to using "obstetric forceps" (1920/1950, p. 208). In addition to believing in the need for more directness on the part of therapists, he also stressed frankness, empathy, and democracy in the patient–therapist relationship (Rachman, 1988), presaging many aspects of object relations, self-psychology, and social justice therapies.

---

[2] I thank Diana Fosha for her permission to use her concept of taboo in this way (personal communication, December 5, 2008).

Otto Rank (1929/1978), a colleague of Ferenczi's, broke two important psychoanalytic taboos. The first was by setting time limits on treatment, initially stemming from his concept of the *birth trauma*. If pathology were not solely due to insufficient resolution of the Oedipal conflict, but also to earlier developmental issues of separation and individuation, then setting time limits could help patients deal with their separation anxieties. The second major brief therapy influence was Rank's assessment of the patient's motivation to change—his concept of *will*. Resistance was no longer seen as something negative to be overcome by interpretation, but rather in a positive light, as a strength of the individual. As Rank's biographer, Jessie Taft (1958) wrote, "the 'will' focus liberated Rank finally from his Freudian past, from the biological developmental details of family history as the core of analytic procedure and from the old psychoanalytic terminology" (p. 145). Because his contributions have formed the backbone of many modern approaches, Marmor (1979) suggested that Rank "may well be the most important historical forerunner of the brief dynamic psychotherapy movement" (p. 150).

In 1925, Ferenczi and Rank published *The Development of Psychoanalysis*, in which they advocated time limits, a focus for the treatment, an active stance for the therapist, and the importance of the patient's emotional experience. Even by today's standards, these authors' contributions to brief dynamic psychotherapy remain innovative and central to current dynamic approaches. If we look at Ferenczi and Rank in terms of psychoanalytic prohibitions, they were bulls in the virtual china shop of taboos. No longer was there an interminable therapy with an emotionally distant therapist. Gone too was the taboo on self-disclosure and authenticity. Needless to say, their views were not greeted warmly by Freud and the established analytic circle, who saw them as threats to the traditional therapeutic stance. This strong negative reaction stultified the previously promising trajectory of brief therapy for many years.

Several years after Freud's death in 1939, another serious challenge to classical psychoanalysis occurred. In their seminal book *Psychoanalytic Therapy: Principles and Applications*, Alexander and French (1946) questioned the presumed relationship between therapeutic outcome and length of therapy. Their suggestions are so specific, and the eventual impact of their book so great, that I consider it to be the first brief therapy manual. Alexander and French challenged the prevailing assumption that it was critical for the analyst to expose repressed memories through interpretation. They felt that psychotherapists should provide their patients with a *corrective emotional experience*. In commenting on a specific case, they conclude:

> The patient had to experience a new father-son relationship before he could release the old one. This cannot be done as an intellectual exercise; it has to be lived through, i.e., felt, by the patient and thus become an integral part of his emotional life. Only then can he change his attitudes. (p. 63)

In addition, Alexander and French advocated therapist flexibility and adjusting the length and frequency of sessions. These maneuvers were intended to prevent the patient's passive dependency and decompensation into acting out strong infantile feelings and conflicts toward the analyst (i.e., transference neurosis). These ideas were met with intense controversy within the psychoanalytic establishment, and as with Rank and Ferenczi, Alexander and French's contributions were ignored for many years. The taboos Alexander and French broke were multifold. As a result, several major, modern therapeutic models can be traced to their ideas of providing a corrective emotional experience and flexibility in therapeutic strategies and treatment length. Grotjahn (1966) extended his observation that if Freud disturbed the sleep of the world, then "Franz Alexander disturbed the sleep of the psychiatrists and psychoanalysts" (p. 390)!

## SECOND GENERATION: SHORT-TERM DYNAMIC PSYCHOTHERAPIES

In this phase, roughly from 1960 to 1980, brief dynamic therapy began to emerge as a legitimate therapeutic method in its own right. David Malan of the Tavistock Clinic in London, Habib Davanloo of Montreal General Hospital in Canada, Peter Sifneos of Massachusetts General Hospital in Boston, and James Mann of Boston University School of Medicine are seen as the main representatives of this second generation. As Messer and

Warren (1995) point out, the aim of the members of this generation was to use psychoanalytic techniques such as interpretation and clarification in ways that would shorten the therapies.

Malan's approach was initially called *focal therapy;* later it was referred to as *intensive brief psychotherapy* (IBP), the first major approach to my knowledge to use the word "brief" (usually taking 20–40 sessions). Malan believed that "far reaching changes could be brought about in relatively severe and chronic illnesses by a technique of active interpretation containing all the essential elements of full scale analysis" (1976, p. 20). Like Ferenczi before him, Malan thought that the analyst's passivity was chiefly responsible for the lengthy analyses and that one way to combat this passivity was to find a focus for the therapy. Malan concentrated on identification of a "focal problem"—a nuclear (childhood) conflict that was manifested in some form in the current presenting problem. He would frame the focal problem in terms of patients' characteristic defense–anxiety–impulse configurations—that is, the characteristic defensive behaviors patients employed to protect themselves from experiencing anxiety-provoking impulses or feelings. Malan referred to this configuration as the *triangle of conflict* and used interpretations to articulate the connections between and among the three components. For example, the therapist might observe that a patient becomes very intellectual whenever she feels anger.

Malan would also draw patients' attention to how they used the same defensive strategies developed in childhood in sessions with the therapist (transference) and with others in their lives. Interpretations connecting emotionally charged interactions with past significant others, present significant others, and one's therapist form what has been called the *triangle of person* or *triangle of insight* (Menninger, 1958). For example, the therapist might point out that a patient's intellectualizing in session seems characteristic of how she handled anxiety as a child. Even though Malan was writing a half-century ago, his description of the need to maintain a focus sounds like a current text for those wanting to learn how to practice brief therapy. "The therapist refuses to be diverted by material irrelevant to the focus, however tempting this may be" (Malan, 1963, p. 210).

In terms of taboo breaking, Malan broke the psychoanalytic taboo on activity and directiveness (Fosha, 1995). He also specifically broke the taboo on limiting the inquiry of the analyst. Here we see explicit permission for the therapist to selectively neglect certain aspects of the clinical material, as fascinating as they might be, if they are not germane to the focus.

Davanloo developed the *intensive short-term dynamic psychotherapy* (ISTDP) approach in the 1960s. ISTDP was designed to break through the patient's defensive barrier using *active, confrontive techniques* in addition to interpretation (Neborsky, 2006). Davanloo challenged not only formal defenses (e.g., projection, rationalization), but also the more tactical, verbal, and nonverbal defenses. For example, he would attack the patient's vagueness, tentativeness, looking away, evasiveness, sighing, rumination, and weepiness. Here instead of interpretation, there was head-on confrontation. Insight into one's defensive posture was not the goal, but rather eradication of defenses so that the patient could release a full range of repressed thoughts, memories, and feelings. "You don't limit yourself to squinting through a peephole when you can walk in through the front door" (Davanloo, as quoted by Fosha, 1995). Davanloo (1978) has a reputation for being "the relentless healer." It is not surprising that he originally was in training to become a surgeon.

Davanloo violated many psychoanalytic prohibitions. He broke particularly sacred taboos requiring neutrality, abstinence, and being "nice" to the patient (Fosha, 1995). He also broke the taboo on keeping what went on in therapy private. He video-recorded ISTDP sessions and scrutinized them to learn what was helpful and what was not.

Sifneos (1979/1987), in his *short-term anxiety-provoking psychotherapy* (STAPP), specified selection and exclusion criteria, used heightened focal inquiry, and actively interpreted and confronted defenses. STAPP concentrates on brief dynamic therapy with relatively high-functioning patients experiencing conflicts associated with Oedipal issues. No number of sessions is agreed on at the outset, but a length between 10 and 20 sessions is determined as the therapy proceeds. Sifneos assumes a role that is part therapist and part teacher; he is "like a schoolmaster seeing through the excuses and alibis of his recalcitrant pupils" (Burke, White, & Havens, 1979, p. 178). For example, a STAPP therapist, after hearing "I don't know" from the patient in response to a question about the patient's emotional ties to her father, says, "Oh, come on, of course you know! Just tell me!" (Nielsen & Barth, 1991, p. 66).

James Mann (1973) is credited with modifying basic psychoanalytic philosophy and techniques by focusing specifically on difficulties dealing with separation and loss (Levenson, Butler, & Bein, 2002), lending a decidedly existential tone. Viewing a sense of timelessness as part of a person's unconscious, Mann designed a time-limited structure for the therapy consisting of 12 sessions—no more, no less. Theoretically, this structure with a precise ending date was designed to help the patient face unconscious wishes for "eternal time," and thereby master separation anxiety in the context of an empathic therapeutic relationship. More dramatically than his brief therapy peers, Mann definitively broke the taboo challenging the concept of the ever-present therapist—a therapist who "will be here as long as you need me."

Clearly contemporary brief therapists owe a debt of gratitude to these second-generation pioneers. But while Malan, Davanloo, Sifneos, and Mann challenged some basic tenets of psychoanalytic theory and practice, they all (to varying degrees) still adhered to the Freudian, intrapsychic (one-person), drive/structural model (Messer & Warren, 1995). From this perspective, sexual and aggressive impulses are viewed as basic drives within the individual, seeking an outlet, with the ego mediating between their push for unbounded expression and internalized societal constraints.

## THIRD GENERATION: RESEARCH-BASED INTERPERSONAL THERAPIES

The approaches of the second generation furthered the practice of brief dynamic psychotherapy, but empirical support for such theories was sparse. Selection criteria and interventions were formulated primarily by ideology, clinical judgment, and theoretical inference, rather than being guided by systematic application of research findings (Perry et al., 1983). The third generation of brief therapies, beginning in the mid-1980s, did much to provide empirical support for the efficacy of brief dynamic therapy as well as to elucidate its active therapeutic ingredients. Furthermore, the third-generation therapies heralded a move away from *intra*psychic (one-person) models of theory and practice to more *inter*personal (two-person) ones. In fact, Messer and Warren (1995) refer to the therapies of this generation as examples of "relational models," because they emphasize the fundamental importance of relationships with others in understanding psychological health and pathology. Representatives of this wave are *time-limited dynamic psychotherapy* (TLDP), developed by Hans Strupp and Jeffrey Binder at Vanderbilt University (1984); *supportive-expressive psychotherapy*, formulated by Lester Luborsky at the University of Pennsylvania (1984); and *control mastery theory*, created by Joseph Weiss and Harold Sampson at Mount Zion Hospital in San Francisco (1986).

The original version of TLDP will be briefly reviewed as both an example of a third-generation model and as the foundation for examining it in greater depth throughout this book. The background for TLDP comes from a program of empirical research begun in the early 1950s. Strupp (1955a, 1955b, 1955c, 1960) found that therapists' interventions reflected their personal (positive or negative) attitude toward clients. His later work (Strupp, 1980) revealed that clients who were hostile, negativistic, inflexible, mistrusting, or otherwise highly resistant uniformly had poor outcomes. Strupp reasoned that these difficult clients had characterological styles that made it very hard for them to negotiate good working relationships with their therapists. In such cases the therapists' skill in managing the interpersonal therapeutic climate was severely taxed, and the therapists became trapped into reacting with negativity, hostility, confusion, and disrespect. Since the therapies were brief, this inability to form a therapeutic alliance quickly had deleterious effects on the entire therapy. These negative effects led Strupp and colleagues to develop TLDP as a method that could help treating professionals maintain their own equilibrium and foster empathy when working with difficult clients.

Personality development and functioning were viewed from an interpersonal and object relations perspective. The major objective of TLDP as originally conceived was to examine *recurrent, maladaptive themes* as evident in the client's interactions with others and with his or her therapist.[3]

---

[3] The reader will note that (except for quotations and historical background material) I begin to use the word *client* here in the text instead of *patient*. This change connotes a shift in psychotherapy in general from a medical model (of passive patient acted upon by The Doctor) to a more relational model in which therapy consists of two people (albeit one of whom is in more emotional pain and one of whom has expertise) who are trying to forge a healing relationship.

Consistent focus was directed to the client's manner of construing and relating to the therapist both as a significant person in the present and as the personification of past relationships (i.e., *transference*). "The TLDP therapist anticipates that (a) troublesome patterns of interpersonal behavior will presently be activated in the patient-therapist relationship; and (b) when an appropriate affective context exists, their hitherto unrecognized meaning can be identified and recast (interpreted)" (Strupp & Binder, 1984, pp. 136–137). The rationale for this approach stemmed from the view that regardless of the severity of psychopathology, interpersonal relations are the arena in which intrapsychic conflict is expressed. A manual for the practice of TLDP, *Psychotherapy in a New Key* (Strupp & Binder, 1984), was published, designed to make the model easier to learn and to standardize the application of TLDP technique.

Five major selection criteria are used in determining a client's appropriateness for TLDP:

- Clients must be in *emotional discomfort* so they are motivated to endure the often challenging and painful change process, and to make sacrifices of time, effort, and money as required by therapy.
- Clients must *come for appointments and engage with the therapist*.
- Clients must be *willing to consider how their relationships have contributed* to distressing symptoms, negative attitudes, and/or behavioral difficulties.
- Clients need to be *willing to examine feelings*.
- Clients should be capable of having a *meaningful relationship* with the therapist.

While these selection criteria are broad based, TLDP would not be appropriate for those whose reality processing is impaired (for example, due to a psychotic thought process, neurological difficulties, or substance abuse) or who present ongoing management issues (e.g., chronic suicidal behavior).

TLDP broke two major psychoanalytic taboos. First was the recognition that the therapist is another living, breathing, interactive person who at times will get pushed and pulled by the client's style of relating, thus recreating *with* the client the dysfunctional dynamic for which the client is seeking help (i.e., *transference–countertransference reenactments*). For Freud and his followers, countertransference had been thought of as a "hindrance to therapy, something to be done away with" (Gelso, 2004, p. 231). It was seen as a manifestation of the therapist's own unconscious, unresolved conflicts that needed to be dealt with in the therapist's own therapy and consultation.

From the TLDP point of view, however, countertransference could be seen as a form of interpersonal empathy, "in which the therapist, for a time and to a limited degree, is recruited into enacting roles assigned to him or her by the patient's preconceived neurotic scenarios" (Strupp & Binder, 1984, p. 149). By finding a way to recognize and to talk directly about these reenactments (metacommunicating), the therapist could help clients have an understanding of their own patterns and their impact. Here we see that the therapist's countertransference can be used to further therapeutic gains rather than being viewed as only detrimental.

This challenged the position of the analyst as someone who is above the fray—an uninvolved, Sherlock Holmes type of detective who is interested in cleverly unearthing the Truth without getting his hands dirty. With TLDP, the therapist gets dirty—because he or she is (for a time) in the rut with the client, with both of them relying on one another to find a way out.

Second, TLDP broke with psychoanalysis by rejecting

> as a major therapeutic goal reconstructions of the past or the recall of repressed memories. . . . From [the TLDP] viewpoint it is not required to reconstruct the patient's history but only to assume that current emotional disturbances and interpersonal difficulties are a product of that history. (Strupp & Binder, 1984, p. 25)

Thus, one can view TLDP as breaking several, major psychoanalytic taboos.

## FOURTH GENERATION: PSYCHODYNAMIC– EXPERIENTIAL TREATMENTS

Contemporary brief dynamic approaches comprising the fourth generation are characterized by three main features. First, they assimilate concepts and/or techniques from a variety of sources external to psychoanalysis (e.g., cognitive–behavior therapy, child development, neuroscience) into the more traditional perspectives and strategies, making them more integrative. Second, they emphasize in-session experiential factors as critical components of the therapeutic process. Third, they are also influenced in the direction of pragmatism and efficiency by powerful economic and sociopolitical forces (Levenson & Burg, 2000).

Examples of brief psychodynamic–integrative approaches are McCullough Vaillant's (1997) *short-term anxiety-regulating psychotherapy* (STARP), which applies principles of learning theory while creating opportunities for intense in-session affective experience; Safran and Muran's (2000) *brief relational therapy* (BRT), which is designed to help therapists recognize and resolve problems in the therapeutic alliance; Fosha's (2000) *accelerated experiential dynamic therapy* (AEDP), which uses explicit empathy and radical therapeutic engagement to promote the clients' own healing affects; and an *integrative, attachment-based, experiential version of TLDP*.

In 1995, I wrote *Time-Limited Dynamic Psychotherapy: A Guide for Clinical Practice.* As the title indicates, that book was designed to translate TLDP principles and strategies into pragmatically useful ways of thinking and intervening for the practitioner. The text contains many examples of how to use TLDP concepts and interventions by providing moment-to-moment, nitty-gritty details of client–therapist interactions in real clinical situations. In that book, I made a substantial shift from that presented in Strupp and Binder's original 1984 conception of TLDP in that I placed a major emphasis on *change through experiential learning* as opposed to insight.

I viewed this experiential learning as the first goal of TLDP; it highlighted the importance of affective–action components of change rather than those that come from cognitive shifts through insight. My view of such experiential learning at the time focused chiefly on modifying the interaction between client and others (initially often the therapist) so that the client had the opportunity to experience trying out new behaviors in the context of a safe enough therapeutic relationship. Could the person have a new experience in the present that would disconfirm his or her expectations of negative responses from others? If one could step forward to engage differently and be responded to differently (i.e., more positively), the anxiety that came with that interpersonal risk gets lessened or alleviated and one becomes encouraged to take other risks, thereby shifting one's entire interpersonal pattern over time. This disconfirmation of the feared expectation follows learning theory principles embedded within a system of complementary interpersonal transactions and results in powerful learning reminiscent of that achieved through exposure treatment.

Imagine that a person who has been competitive and dominant his whole life takes a risk to be more vulnerable and dependent in the therapy and experiences a sense of relief when his therapist does not take advantage of him. With enough repetitions over time and with other people, he is encouraged to be increasingly more collaborative with others; eventually his off-putting dominant style softens, inviting others to be more connected to him.

Since writing my 1995 text, my belief about the central role of experiential learning has only been strengthened and broadened. During that time, the field of affective neuroscience has burgeoned and the role of emotion has moved to center stage (Schore, 2009). We are learning more about how we are hard-wired to maintain interpersonal connectedness and how much of what makes us feel safe in the world is communicated in subtle but powerful moments when we sense someone is affectively attuned to us (Cosolino, 2006). The TLDP model set forth in this book highlights the need for affective attunement and evocative empathy along with promoting new interpersonal experiences (and new understandings) to foster healthier interpersonal and intrapersonal functioning.

TLDP has many attractive features. It does not emphasize pathology but rather sees that the client is doing the best he or she can. It has broad selection criteria so many challenging clients are accepted for treatment. As it addresses fundamental shifts intrapsychically and interpersonally, psychodynamically trained therapists can use it without giving up their allegiance to "depth-work." In addition, it is one of the few short-term approaches that has studied how therapists *learn* a specific brief model of therapy (Henry et al., 1993a, 1993b). TLDP is rather jargon-free and avoids inferential concepts with unclear referents. Although the approach is clearly psychodynamic in origin, it does not view the individual as needing to work through childhood conflicts in therapy. Rather the client's problems are seen as being maintained in the present through a dynamic system of maladaptive behaviors and self-defeating interpersonal expectations that "invite" the very response from others most feared by the client.

Fourth-generation brief dynamic models clearly broke the taboo of theoretical and strategic purity—they have become the mutts of the psychodynamic kennel. They do not look as elegant and refined as the purebreds. They have so welcomed ideas, strategies, and therapeutic stances from other models to jump the fence that it sometimes becomes quite difficult to clearly discern their "psychodynamic" lineage. However, what they give up in uniformity and grace, they more than make up for in their robustness and hardiness (and "heartiness" as well). They seem vital and flexible, able to adapt to the needs of their various owners at various times. They are also friendly and inviting—even welcoming positive experience over painful lessons (Fosha, 2000). It certainly is not your grandfather's brief dynamic psychotherapy. However, at the base of these current brief psychotherapies, one can still make out the traditional importance placed on the role of conflict, unconscious processes, transference, countertransference, and the regulation of anxiety common to all psychodynamic models. In the ensuing chapters, my integrative version of time-limited dynamic psychotherapy will be examined in depth to elucidate the theory, formulation, process, and application of a current fourth-generation model of brief dynamic psychotherapy.

# Theory

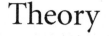

The integrative view of time-limited dynamic psychotherapy (TLDP) intertwines three substantive approaches that have complex, overlapping historic and clinical perspectives, each one pertaining to a different focus of the clinical work. The first leg of this theoretical stool is *attachment theory,* which provides the motivational rationale for the therapy. From attachment theory, one can answer the questions "Why do people behave as they do?" "What is necessary for mental health, and how does mental illness occur?" The second support comes from *interpersonal–relational theory,* which forms the frame or platform for the therapy. "What is the medium in which the therapy occurs?" The third leg emphasizes the *experiential– affective component,* which is concerned with the process of change. "What needs to shift for change to occur?" When I am working clinically, I experienced these three perspectives as inseparable and reinforcing one another— all contributing to support a stable base from which to do therapy.[1] In the

---

[1] Each of these three components has been identified as an empirically supported, therapeutic change principle in the modern practice of psychotherapy (e.g., Castonguay & Beutler, 2005; Neborsky, 2006).

next section each component will be examined so that the reader can better understand my current perspectives on the theory and practice of TLDP.

## ATTACHMENT THEORY

### Attachment in Infancy

Attachment theory maintains that infants manifest an instinctive behavioral repertoire (the attachment behavioral system) in the service of maintaining physical closeness to caregivers. From an attachment perspective, we are hardwired to gravitate toward "older and wiser" others particularly during times of stress or threat. Moreover, we are genetically programmed to solicit attention from our caregivers on whom we are dependent because our very existence depends on this vital bond. Infants' ability to elicit such attention is then maintained through a *mutual feedback loop* in which caregivers (usually initially mothers) are socially reinforced by their infants for engaging in attentional behaviors (e.g., the infant's steady gaze reinforces the mother's cooing and staring back, which then encourages the infant to fixate on her face and engage in smiling behaviors that again results in more rapt attention from mother). There is ample research to indicate that some of an infant's ability to imitate the social behavior of another (e.g., stick out one's tongue after seeing the mother stick out her tongue) and to respond to social cues from a caregiver are not learned and are already available in the infant's behavioral repertoire just a few hours after birth (Meltzoff & Moore, 1977).

The literature on attachment theory and its application to understanding human development is enormous and spans nearly 40 years (Obegi & Berant, 2008). John Bowlby's classic trilogy on attachment, separation, and loss (1969, 1973, 1980) highlighted the importance of the emotional quality of early childhood for understanding psychopathology. Through observations, consultations, and the empirical/theoretical literature that existed at the time, Bowlby concluded that

> the young child's hunger for his [sic] mother's love and presence is as great as his hunger for food, and that in consequence her absence inevitably generates a powerful sense of loss and anger. . . . Thus

we reached the conclusion that loss of mother-figure, either by itself or in combination with other variables yet to be clearly identified, is capable of generating responses and processes that are of the greatest interest to psychopathology. (1969, p. xiii)[2]

Bowlby noticed that infants had a large repertoire of behaviors to keep their mothers close and interactive. He believed the infant had acquired this behavioral repertoire gradually over the course of evolution; those infants who could connect had a better chance of passing on their DNA to future generations. "Bowlby viewed the human infant's reliance on, and emotional bond with, its mother to be the result of a *fundamental instinctual behavioral system* that, unlike Freud's sexual libido concept, was relational without being sexual" (Mikulincer & Shaver, 2007, p. 7, emphasis added).

## Attachment Patterns

While attachment originally pertained to an infant's proximity seeking, Bowlby later wrote of how the attachment needs and behaviors continue throughout the life cycle, with adults turning to other adults, especially in times of stress. As he stated in his treatise on healthy human development, *A Secure Base* (1988), "All of us, *from the cradle to the grave*, are happiest when life is organized as a series of excursions, long or short, from the secure base provided by our attachment figure(s)" (emphasis added, p. 62). We probably have no stronger example of this in modern times than when so many people in the Twin Towers on 9/11, when faced with a certain, horrific death, reached for their cell phones for the sole purpose of making contact with loved ones.

The analysts called Bowlby a behaviorist (the ultimate condemnation, no doubt) because of his interest in animal research and in observing the actual behavior of children. But quite to the contrary, the behaviorists would have nothing to do with his ideas. During this time, John Watson, for example, was cautioning parents not to reward crying children with

---

[2] When Bowlby heard Harry Harlow speak at an American Psychological Association Convention in 1958, he immediately saw the relevancy of Harlow's work with rhesus monkeys who preferred a "cloth mother," even though they were fed by a wire mesh "mother" (Karen, 1998).

attention. "Never hug and kiss them . . . never let them sit in your lap. If you must, kiss them once on the forehead when they say goodnight" (Watson, 1928, as quoted by Lewis, Amini, & Lannon, 2001, p. 71).

Ainsworth, an American colleague of Bowlby's, developed an experimental procedure to assess the attachment patterns of infants called the "Strange Situation" (Ainsworth, 1969). In this situation, infants came with their mothers into a room with a one-way mirror. The infants would spend some time in the room with their mothers, an experimenter, and a variety of toys. At some point the mother would leave the child alone with the experimenter who recorded the child's behavior. When the mother came back a short time later, the child's behavior was again noted. Infants who were classified as *secure* were able to use their mothers as a home base as they explored their new surroundings. When their mothers left, they were obviously distressed, but they were able to be soothed by her return and resume constructive play. Children who were classified as *avoidant* exhibited little visible distress when their mothers left and did not greet her upon her return. They seemed more interested in the toys, but their play was not particularly creative.[3] These children were thought to have deactivated their attachment system. The children labeled as *anxious-ambivalent* looked distressed even when they entered the room with their mothers. When their mothers left, they cried and were visibly angry. At reunion, these children were not able to be comforted and remained hyperaroused, unable to return to their play activities.

## Internal Working Models

Bowlby's formulations about the significance of internal working models help therapists understand how patterns of attachment might be maintained over time.[4] He postulated that "an internal psychological organiza-

---

[3] It should be noted that while the avoidant children did not appear distressed, measurements of their physiology showed high degrees of activation. Thus, with children and adults classified as avoidant, there is often marked internal distress with behavioral suppression.

[4] According to Mikulincer and Shaver (2007), the term *working* models was to connote two ideas: (1) the models are heuristic—that is, they are pragmatically useful in predicting likely outcomes, and (2) the models are provisional—that is, they are changeable as in a *working* title (p. 15).

tion with a number of highly specific features, which include representational models of the self and of attachment figure(s)" (1988, p. 29) develops over time and is built up through a series of experiences with caregivers throughout one's early life. Thus the child not only has an internalized set of expectancies about how he or she will be treated by others, but also an internalized model of how one sees, feels about, and treats one's self that is a reflection of how one has been treated by others.

Bowlby postulated that a securely attached child (i.e., a child who has been responded to by caregivers in a contingent, helpful, and loving manner whether distressed or contented) comes to expect that there are no aspects of the self that cannot be noticed, responded to, and dealt with. However, children who are not securely attached (i.e., who have been responded to sporadically, noncontingently, inadequately, or inappropriately) learn that when they are under threat, they cannot count on others to keep them safe.

Insecurely attached children get a quadruple whammy. First, they have models of self and/or others that are negative; second, they also have considerable difficulty self-correcting these harmful internalized models because of difficulties cognitively and emotionally perceiving disconfirmatory incoming information; third, since their working models or templates are derived and perpetuated out of awareness, they continue to be at their mercy. I am reminded of the saying that a fish has no idea of water. So it is with working models. They have an enormous impact on our lives, but we take them for granted as the way life is. Wachtel (2008) points out a fourth way insecurely attached children are affected. The stability of their internal working models persists in part because the ongoing interactions with the very people who gave rise to these experiences also persist (e.g., parents who were harsh toward their child as an infant are harsh when the child is a toddler and harsh when the child is an adolescent).

## Adult Attachment

How does one understand the relevancy of attachment theory for adults? As Bowlby stated, attachment is significant from "cradle to grave," but by the time people are adults, they normally do not need the proximity to another human being to survive. Adults feel secure when their attachment figures have confirmed "that (a) they are loved and lovable people, and (b) they are competent or have mastery over their environment" (Pietromonaco & Feldman Barrett, 2000, p. 167). Over the years, this builds up a sense of *felt security* that individuals internalize and carry with them throughout the lifespan (Stroufe & Waters, 1977).

Shaver and Mikulincer (2008) delineate the three critical functions necessary for a person to reach adult attachment figure status: (a) this person is sought out at times of stress, or this person's undesired leaving creates distress and protest; (b) this person creates a "safe haven" because he/she is a source of comfort, protection, or security; and (c) this person provides a "secure base" from which the adult can explore the world, take risks, and pursue self-development. Bowlby (1969/1982) acknowledged that a variety of people, personages (like God), or even institutions could be seen as attachment figures. In addition, the mental representations of these central figures (or of oneself) also can be a source of felt security and comfort. In a series of ingenious studies (see Shaver & Mikulincer, 2008), it has been demonstrated that activation of mental representations of attachment figures (e.g., asking people to visualize the faces of such figures) promotes a positive feeling, reduces painful or hurt feelings, and fosters empathy. (As a mini-experiment right now, the reader could take a moment and imagine seeing the face of someone who has provided comfort and security. Are you aware of having more positive feelings and an increased sense of well-being?)

Mary Main, a student of Ainsworth's, developed the Adult Attachment Interview (AAI; Main, Kaplan, & Cassidy, 1985) to explore the mental representations of adults' attachment as children to their parents. The AAI asks people to respond to specific questions about their relationships with their parents when they were young. For example, "Could you give me five adjectives or phrases to describe your relationship with your mother during childhood?" Those interviewed are then classified into one of three attachment styles—secure, dismissing, or preoccupied—corresponding to the three categories found for infants in the Strange Situation.

Secure adults describe their pasts (even those that were distressing) in a clear and coherent manner; dismissing adults give few examples of their relationships with parents and offer sparse, minimizing responses (e.g., "My relationship with my mother was fine"); and preoccupied adults' responses show an inability to pull back from their anger and/or anxiety, apparently overwhelmed by their feelings. Thus, the securely attached individuals demonstrate *autobiographical competence* (Holmes, 1993; Siegel, 1999); they are able to tell a coherent story of how the past affected them and why they are the way they are. Furthermore, they are able to *mentalize* (Fonagy & Target, 2006); they can "interpret others' minds, which in turn fostered the ability to read and understand one's own mental states, especially those mental states that are based on emotions" (Jurist & Meehan, 2008, p. 72). Such autobiographical competence and the ability to mentalize have been hypothesized to be central to affect regulation and mental health in general.[5]

## Attachment-Based Therapy

Although there is no specific "attachment therapy" for adults, the relevance of attachment theory for therapeutic formulation and intervention is enormous. Bowlby (1988) outlined five therapeutic tasks—all revolving around the therapist's role of providing "conditions in which his [sic] patient can explore his representational models of himself and his attachment figures with a view to reappraising and restructuring them in the light of the *new understanding* he acquires and the *new experiences* he has in the therapeutic relationship" (emphasis added, p. 138). Specifically, the therapist must: (a) provide a secure base, a "trusted companion," so that the painful aspects of one's life can be examined; (b) assist exploration of expectations and biases in forming connections with others; (c) encourage consideration of how early parenting experiences are related to current functioning; (d) help the patient see the past for what it is and help him or her to imagine healthier alternative ways of acting and thinking; and (e) help examine the therapeutic relationship as the patient's working models of self and other play out in the therapy. In fact, Bowlby felt that examining the transference and countertransference in the here and now of the sessions should be the

---

[5] Siegel and Hartzell (2003) wrote a book for parents to help them understand that they could promote their children's mental health by "making sense" of their own lives in a way that is coherent—a way that tells a story of how the past affected them and why they are the way they are in the present. Siegel (1999) believes that such coherence leads to neural integration and facilitates raising securely attached children.

main focus of therapy, with explorations of the patient's past delved into only as they are useful in helping one understand current ways of feeling and coping with one's interpersonal world. It is in this context that Bowlby specifically mentioned the work of Strupp and Binder (1984) in his 1988 book, *A Secure Base*, stating that TLDP contains many of the same ideas on therapeutic process that he has outlined.

## INTERPERSONAL–RELATIONAL THEORY
### Harry Stack Sullivan

The relational approach is a potentially confusing one to discuss because there is not a "relational school" per se. However, most writers on the topic credit Sullivan in the 1940s for first bringing to light the relevancy of the interpersonal dimension for psychotherapy. Sullivan challenged the then-prevalent Freudian position that viewed the discharge of biological drives as determining the development of personality; instead, he maintained that an innate push for interpersonal relatedness was pivotal.

In the introduction to his now-classic book, *The Psychiatric Interview* (1954), Sullivan made it very clear:

> *Psychiatry is defined as the field of study of interpersonal relations,* emphasis being placed on the interaction of the participants in a social situation rather than being centered exclusively on the supposedly private economy of either one of those participants. (emphasis added, p. ix)

In fact, Sullivan saw personality as "that relatively enduring pattern of *recurrent interpersonal situations* which characterize the human life" (emphasis added, 1953, p. 111). Children develop, through interactions with their parents, a sense of self–other role relationship patterns that later result in interpersonal coping styles—strategies that are designed to avoid or manage anxiety and maintain a modicum of self-esteem.

Initially through his work with patients diagnosed as schizophrenic, Sullivan studied difficulties people have in understanding what someone else "means." He became fascinated with what gets communicated in interactions and used a voice-recording machine in an attempt to discern what had happened in sessions—not only the words, but also the non-linguistic aspects of speech. As early as the mid-1920s, he also proposed photographing sessions so that one could view the nonverbal components in interactions, such as gestures and body positioning (Sullivan, 1927).

Because Sullivan viewed the therapeutic encounter as occurring within a social field, he commented not only on the anxiety of the patient, but also on the anxiety of the therapist, and he emphasized the critical importance of emotions for understanding current therapeutic transactions. He saw that the therapist was far from a neutral observer:

> The psychiatrist cannot stand off to one side and apply his sense organs, however, they may be refined by the use of apparatus, to noticing what someone else does, without becoming personally implicated in the operation. . . . The processes and the changes in processes that make up the data . . . occur, not in the subject person nor in the observer, but in the situation which is created *between the observer and his subject.* (emphasis added, 1954, p. 3)

For Sullivan, therapeutic sessions consisted of a "two-group." He explained that although the number of people in the room might only be two, "the number of more or less imaginary people that get themselves involved in this two-group is sometimes really hair-raising" (1954, p. 9). Sullivan coined the term *participant observer* to describe how the therapist on the one hand is the expert observer, noting what is going on in the session, and on the other hand and at the same time is a full participant in the interaction as another human being.

### Interpersonal Diagnosis

Sullivan's groundbreaking work influenced many who followed, among them Carl Rogers, Erik Erikson, Hans Strupp, Donald Kiesler, and Don Jackson. Some interpersonal theoreticians expanded Sullivan's ideas to map an entire range of interpersonal behaviors onto an interpersonal circle (or circumplex) anchored by the two orthogonal dimensions of affiliation–disaffiliation and independence–dependence (e.g., Wiggins, 1979; Benjamin, 1974). It was thought that one could locate any interpersonal behavior (in therapy and in the outside world) somewhere on that circle's surface. For example, a friendly (high on affiliation) submissive (high on dependence) person's behavior could be located in a particular quadrant of the circumplex. Such classifications also led to delineating more precisely how each person's behavior might influence another person's behavior.

Empirical research and clinical observation (Horowitz & Strack, in press) support that hostile behavior begets hostility; friendly behavior invites a friendly response; dominant behavior encourages the complementary behavior of submission, and vice versa, submissive behavior invites dominance. For example, our friendly-submissive person's deferring behavior sets the stage for others to respond in friendly-dominant ways (e.g., advising). Thus a subtle shift is occurring here. The therapist's focus is no longer solely on the individual's separate behavior, but rather on the interaction that gets co-created between two or more individuals. The empirical literature on complementarity and dimensionality is quite extensive (Sadler, Woody, & Ethier, in press). These factors have been found to exist across cultures and are quite robust.

Benjamin (1974, 1993) furthered the sophistication and clinical relevancy of interpersonal mapping by developing a multidimensional model and assessment tool of interpersonal *and* intrapsychic interactions—a form of interpersonal diagnosis called the Structural Analysis of Social Behavior (SASB). The SASB is a system of three interrelated circumplex surfaces each described by the two dimensions of affiliation–disaffiliation and independence–interdependence: (1) actions toward another—*focus on other* (e.g., attacking); (2) personal responses to behaviors from others—*focus on the self* (e.g., recoiling); and (3) intrapsychic actions toward oneself—*focus on introject* (e.g., self-rejecting). Observers rate moment-to-moment interactions between two people (husband–wife, parent–child, therapist–client), or individuals can describe their relationships and intrapsychic states via a questionnaire. (See Chapter 5 for information on studies using the SASB.)

Understanding the critical role of interpersonal communication has many implications for understanding what maintains psychopathology (i.e., reverberating negative feedback loops about self and other) and for determining the focus in psychotherapy (i.e., shifting interpersonal patterns of relating). Horowitz and Vitkus (1986) examined the interpersonal basis of psychiatric symptoms to elucidate how these vicious cycles of relating might function in maintaining mental illness. For example, a depressed person seeks help from others from a submissive and helpless position. Others are pulled to react from a position of dominance and might try to help by advising the person what he or she should do to get better. This more dominant stance, unfortunately, encourages more submissiveness from the depressed individual and thereby serves to reinforce his or her depression, completing the vicious cycle.

Allen Frances (former Chair of the DSM-IV Task Force) wrote the foreword to Benjamin's book *Interpersonal Diagnosis and Treatment of Personality Disorders* (1993). His opening paragraph captures best the attitude of the interpersonal therapist.

> The essence of being a mammal (and, most essentially, we are mammals) is the need for, and the ability to participate in, interpersonal relationships. The interpersonal dance begins at least as early as birth and ends only with death. . . . There are very few human activities, including psychotherapy, that are not best considered and defined from within an interpersonal model. (p. v)

## Two-Person Perspective

This interpersonal perspective reflects a larger paradigm shift occurring within psychoanalytic thinking and practice that has usually been framed as the one-person (focus within) versus two-person (focus between) paradigm. Messer and Warren (1995) comment that most psychoanalytic schools are becoming less drive-oriented and more relational for various cultural, social, clinical, and scientific reasons. Not only within psychoanalysis but in other models of psychotherapy as well (e.g., cognitive therapy, Safran & Segal, 1990; behavior therapy, Kohlenberg & Tsai, 1991), there is a growing incorporation of interpersonal perspectives.

For the practicing clinician this shift to a more relational stance affects what gets defined as pathology, how one formulates the case, how the therapist construes the present clinical situation, what interventions are considered most helpful, and how outcome is evaluated. It is beyond the scope of this chapter to describe all of the epistemological, conceptual, and procedural differences between one-person and two-person approaches, but Table 3.1 lists most of the major ones.

## Table 3.1   One-Person vs. Two-Person Paradigms in Psychoanalytic Thought and Practice

| One Person | Two-Person |
|---|---|
| **Model** | |
| Drive–Conflict Model | Relational Model |
| Conflict between instinctual impulses and societal demands | Conflict between attachment needs and environmental requirements |
| Linear cause and effect | Reciprocal influences |
| Intrapsychic | Interpersonal; interactional |
| Minimize cultural determinants | Embedded in a cultural context |
| **Role of Therapist** | |
| Objective translator; decoder; decipherer | Participant–observer; total participant |
| Neutral screen; blank screen | Coparticipant; inevitable embeddedness of therapist in relationship matrix |
| **Transference** | |
| Transference as distortion | Therapist's actual behavior strongly affects client |
| **Countertransference** | |
| Countertransference as failure to remain neutral | Neutrality as an impossible position for the therapist |
| Product of therapist's unresolved conflicts and childhood residues | Interpersonal empathy |
| **Strategy/Technique** | |
| Accurate interpretation; emphasis on content and precision | Corrective emotional experience |
| Interpretation as truth revealing hidden content | Narrative as truth; a way of understanding (one of several) |
| Communication made explicit | Implicit relational knowing |
| **View of Client** | |
| Reactive | Active construer of interpersonal world |

From Alexander & French (1945); Aron (1991); Beebe & Lachman (1988); Bowlby (1973); Burke (1992); Cooper (1987); Eagle (1984); Emde (1991); Fenichel (1941); Gabbard (1993); Gill (1982); Greenberg (1991); Hirsch (1992); Hoffman (1992); Mitchell (1988); Ogden (1994); Sandler (1976); Stern (2004); Strupp & Binder (1984); Sullivan (1953); Wachtel (2008); Weiss et al. (1986); Wolf (1986); Wolstein (1983).

Adapted from *Time-Limited Dynamic Psychotherapy: A Guide to Clinical Practice*, by H. Levenson, 1995, and reprinted here with permission of Basic Books, a member of the Perseus Book Group.

As pointed out by Pincus and Ansell (2003) in their chapter on the interpersonal theory of personality, the presence of others and how they foster interpersonal learning has implications for self-regulation, field regulation, and affect regulation, which brings us to the final leg of our theoretical stool—experiential–affective learning.

## EXPERIENTIAL–AFFECTIVE THEORY

Experiential learning through affect is of paramount importance to an understanding of TLDP because it focuses on the crucial change agent part of the model. Focusing on affect and the expression of emotion has long been a key feature of psychodynamic psychotherapies (Hilsenroth, 2007). However, we have learned much in recent years about the nature of emotion.

Emotion theorists (e.g., Frijda, 1986; Lazarus, 1991; Tomkins, 1963) have underscored the function of emotion as adaptive, organizing, and motivating—preparing the organism for action and direction, while also serving expressive and communicative functions—to oneself as well as to others. From what we know about the bidirectionality of the brain and behavior, our brain can generate emotion, our bodies can give emotional signals to the brain, and our behaviors can heighten or dampen our emotional reactivity. Developmental researchers and neuroscientists (e.g., Damasio, 1999; Ekman & Davidson, 1994; LeDoux, 1996; Panksepp, 1998) in particular have greatly expanded what we know about emotions and feelings.

While psychodynamically oriented therapists have always paid attention to the emotional life of their clients, now practitioners and theorists from other orientations, including cognitive–behavioral (Barlow, 2000; Burum & Goldfried, 2007), are acknowledging the central role of emotions in creating change. In fact, Schore (2009) has claimed we are in an "emotion revolution." He opines that within psychology there has been a focus on behavioral and then cognitive approaches in the 20th century, but that there will be an increasing emphasis on emotion for understanding therapeutic change in the 21st. Our ability to scan and map what is going on in our brains through functional magnetic resonance imaging (fMRI), positron emission tomography (PET scans), and single photon emission computed tomography (SPECT) have greatly increased our knowledge base and pushed our theorizing about emotion and its relationship to psychotherapy even further (Frewen, Dozois, & Lanius, 2008; Peres & Nasello, 2007).

## Felt Sense

However, we are not always consciously aware of our feelings. Helping clients become aware of, experience, and process emotions (Greenberg, Rice, & Elliott, 1993, p. 42) is a crucial part of experiential therapies. Damasio (1999), in his thoughtful book titled appropriately *The Feeling of What Happens*, sees that our initial ways of knowing are as a felt, bodily sense. In addition, neuroscientists speculate that early experiences (especially traumatic experiences) that occur before the advent of language are stored in what has been called implicit or emotional memory. Schore (2004) discusses neurobiological studies suggesting that development of the right hemisphere is more advanced than that of the left through the second year of life. This might help us understand why early events are not recalled as consciously, linguistically cued memories (a function predominantly of the left hemisphere); rather they are "remembered" as sensations or feelings. This has enormous implications for how a therapist might need to facilitate a client's "felt sense" (Gendlin, 1996) in the therapeutic work.

Thus, from the experiential–affective point of view, the ubiquitous therapist question, "And how do you feel about that?" should more accurately be, "*And how or where do you feel that?*" With estimates that over 60% of all human communication is nonverbal (Burgoon, 1985), a therapist must be quite attentive to moment-to-moment fluctuations of facial expression, tones of voice, postural shifts, and so on within the therapeutic dyad to be able to understand even a small piece of what is being transmitted.[6]

---

[6]Not only do therapists need to become aware of how clients are communicating with them nonverbally, they also must become aware of how they are sending nonverbal signals to clients. Videotaping sessions, especially close-ups of the therapist, is invaluable in this regard.

## Emotional Regulation

Being emotionally aware, emotionally intelligent (Goleman, 1995), emotionally reprocessed (Linehan, 1993), and emotionally regulated (Schore, 1994) have recently been emphasized as signs of mental health. We need to be aware of what our emotions tell us, but it is not enough to just "feel our feelings." We need to be able to regulate (down-shift or up-shift) our emotional experience and expression. Who has not had the experience of counting to 10 in order to calm oneself?

Many (e.g., Fonagy, Gergely, Jurist, & Target, 2002; Siegel, 2007) have suggested that the ability to emotionally regulate oneself is heavily (but fortunately, not solely) influenced by one's early experiences with caregivers. Parents who can attune to their child's emotional state and are able to "metabolize" the child's feelings enable the child to "develop the regulatory circuits in the brain . . . that give the individual a source of resilience as he or she grows. This resilience takes the form of the capacity for self-regulation and engagement with others in empathic relationships" (Siegel, 2007, p. 27). This is a profound idea! Not only does early attunement lead to a healthy psychological life, it may actually lead to the development of healthy brain structures and function and, therefore, to improved interpersonal and intrapsychic functioning. Moreover, when these emotionally regulated children mature and have children of their own, they in turn may foster healthy brain structures and function in their offspring, leading to the next generation's resilience. It is the gift that keeps on giving. And as if that is not enough, there is beginning evidence that psychotherapy can also positively influence these same brain structures and function (e.g., Baxter et al., 1992; Goldapple et al., 2004).

An increasing number of therapists who previously defined themselves as classically psychodynamic (i.e., fostering insight through interpretation) are now placing themselves in the "experiential camp" (Neborsky, 2006, p. 526). Emotion-focused therapy (Greenberg, 2002), emotionally focused couple therapy (Greenberg & Johnson, 1988; Johnson, 2004), and accelerated experiential dynamic psychotherapy (Fosha, 2000) are examples of therapeutic approaches that acknowledge the central role of affect regulation in fostering therapeutic change.

Need to
research

Greenberg and colleagues (Greenberg, 2002; Greenberg & Paivio, 1997; Greenberg & Safran, 1987; Greenberg et al., 1993) have been working for the past 25 years to help clients learn how not only to access emotion within the session but more importantly how to reflect on the meaning of that arousal in the context of a positive therapeutic alliance. In this process–experiential approach to change, Greenberg sets as his goal helping clients "become aware and make productive use of their emotions" (2004, p. 3). Johnson (2004; Johnson et al., 2005), a former student of Greenberg's, has done substantial theoretical and empirical work applying emotionally focused therapy to the treatment of couples, incorporating an attachment lens. Fosha (2000) views the purpose of therapy as helping the client process emotions to completion in order to promote positive feelings such as interest, curiosity, hope, and excitement. Research has shown that depth of emotional experiencing in therapy has been related to positive outcomes (see Whelton, 2004).

## SUMMARY

Bowlby's developmentally rich ideas about internal working models (from attachment theory) have been heated up by the charged nature of emotions (from experiential–affective theory) to better understand the crucial role of transactions with others (interpersonal theory). Hopefully, the reader will now be able to see how the three theoretical aspects on which TLDP rests—attachment theory, the relational perspective, and an experiential–affective focus—merge to form an internally consistent, interlocking network highlighting the essential roles of early relational experiences, dyadic emotional regulation and attunement, present interpersonal transactions, process over content, and here-and-now interpersonal and intrapersonal learning. In the next section I will present the basic premises and goals of this fourth generation brief dynamic therapy model.

*Keep these in → Type + print out
mind * the principles + goals to review
## TLDP PRINCIPLES & reflect on

Nine basic principles are central to TLDP:

1. **People are innately motivated to search for and maintain human relatedness.**

   In TLDP the search for and maintenance of human relatedness is considered to be a major motivating force within all human beings. According to attachment theory, we are hardwired to gravitate toward others.

2. **Maladaptive relationship patterns are acquired early in life, become schematized, and underlie many presenting complaints.**

   How we relate as adults often has its roots in our early relationships with caregivers.[7] These experiences result in mental representations of these relationships or working models of one's interpersonal world. They form the building blocks of what will become organized, encoded, experiential, affective, and cognitive data ("interpersonal schemes"[8]) informing the child about the nature of human relatedness, one's own sense of self, and the actions necessary to get and maintain attention from others. The child then filters the world through the lenses of these interlocking networks. The encoding that takes place at the preverbal level before the child has learned language is made up of sensations, shifts in bodily states, images, smells, or the aforementioned "felt sense."

   └→These would be interesting to access in session

---

[7] While faulty interpersonal styles are usually learned early in life, there are instances where experiences (especially traumatic ones) as an adult may dramatically alter one's working model or even cause irreversible brain damage (Van der Kolk, McFarlane, & Weisath, 1996).

[8] In my previous writings I used the word *schema* or *schemata* to reflect the internal working model (Bowlby, 1988) that individuals hold representing the complex functioning network of thoughts, feelings, and behaviors based upon their attachment experiences. I like the idea of using the word *scheme*, as suggested by Greenberg, Rice, and Elliott (1993), because it conveys the idea of action and process rather than structure. But the term in our society also connotes cunning and deception, and for this reason I do not use it and rely on *schema* or *working model*. Hopefully the reader will keep in mind that when I use these terms, I do not mean a static template, but rather a dynamic process leading to action.

For example, a former client of mine (Mr. Johnson) had parents who treated him in an authoritarian and harsh manner. Consequently, as a young boy, he became overly placating and deferential because it was a way he could stay connected to them. His early experiences led him to expect that others would treat him badly if he were not compliant. Since his meekness led to a certain level of safety (where he avoided being beaten or humiliated), it reinforced and strengthened his internalized working model of how his interpersonal world functioned. While his behaviors, expectations, and self-image served an adaptive purpose as a child, Mr. Johnson entered therapy as an adult because he had no friends, lived a life filled with sense of dread and depression, and could not assert himself. Furthermore, his sense of himself as a loser was evidenced in his slumped shoulders and frequent long sighs. I will return to my work with Mr. Johnson throughout this book as an example of how this brief dynamic therapy model can work with a client with a chronic, pervasive, dysfunctional style.

3. **Relationship patterns persist because they are maintained in current relationships and are consistent with the person's sense of self and other (circular causality).**

From a TLDP framework, the individual's personality is not fixed at a certain point but dynamically changes as he or she interacts with others. While a dysfunctional interactive style may begin early in life, it must be reinforced throughout the person's life for the interpersonal difficulties to continue. What does this look like?

We understand how Mr. Johnson's submissive style started off as a "strategy" to achieve a modicum of safety with his parents. From a TLDP point of view, however, Mr. Johnson's subservient behaviors and self-image would be maintained only to the extent that he can fill his interpersonal world with others who behave toward him in somewhat authoritarian and punitive ways or where the behavior of others is ambiguous enough that he can interpret it according to his own worldview. How does this occur?

Kiesler (1996) in his principles of human communication stipulates that in interaction, one person's message to another "imposes

a condition of emotional engagement" (p. 207). We are prepro-
grammed to respond to such cues based on our emotional hardwiring
combined with what we have learned from our lived experience. Since
Mr. Johnson acts in a subservient manner, as an adult he evokes, pro-
vokes, or invites people (again, usually out of awareness and usually at
a nonverbal level) to behave toward him in a more overbearing manner. When confronted with the oppressive responses of others, Mr.
Johnson feels more "at home" because others' domineering behavior
confirms his internalized view of himself—his self as it has been
reflected in the appraisals of others over time. It feels familiar (feels
"right") when his submissive style dovetails with others' dominance
partly because it operates according to the principles of interpersonal
complementarity and his own emotionally based schemata.

Mr. Johnson is not behaving masochistically by "soliciting" such
transactions. Rather, his submissive way of being in the world is *confirmed* by the dominant responses of others. The real danger inherent
in such transactions and the reason they are so problematic is that
they are derived and perpetuated out of conscious awareness. Furthermore, the unconsciousness, visceral nature of these interpersonal
dances makes it much more difficult to access through explicit verbal
exchanges that usually make up the fabric of discourse in therapy.

Because these implicit relational strategies reflect such core
attachment fears and longings, we run the risk of engaging in an
endless series of self-fulfilling prophecies, resulting in the illusion
that this is just the way life is and that it is "unrealistic" (or totally
unconsidered) to expect something different. The problem is com-
pounded because these compromise solutions often result in real
deficits—deficits in interactive skills, emotional intelligence, and
even the ability to be organized and coherent about one's own mental processes, which as pointed out earlier, can have devastating consequences for generations to come.

This emphasis on the present has tremendous implications for
treating these interpersonal difficulties in a brief time frame. If such
dysfunctional interactions and the internal working models that
fuel them are sustained in the present, then the therapist can work

in the present to make changes at the level of the person's interpersonal interactions (affective–behavioral), negative expectancies
(cognitive), or experience of self (feelings). Consider what might
happen if the others in Mr. Johnson's life did not treat him in such
an authoritarian manner—if they could resist the affective pull
from his submissive style. Also what might happen if those parts of
Mr. Johnson's emotional life that were disowned and blocked at an
early age could be made available to his awareness, expressed, and
reflected on (Greenberg & Pascual-Leone, 2006)? Change could also
occur from the inside out.

*[handwritten marginal note: What does that look like in the therapy room?]*

This focus on transactions in the here-and-now is consistent
with a systems-oriented approach; the context of a problem and the
circular processes surrounding it are critical. The "pathology" does
not reside within an individual but rather is created by all the parts
of the (pathological) system. According to systems theory (Bertalanffy, 1969), if you change one part of the system, the other parts
correspondingly shift.

4. **Therefore, in TLDP, clients are viewed as stuck, not sick.**[9]

Clients are seen as trapped in a rut that they helped dig, not as
deficient. The viewpoint of TLDP is that the clients are in that rut
for the same reason soldiers dig foxholes in war—for self-protection.
The goal of therapy is to help them get out of that hole and put
down their rifles—to give themselves the opportunity to see what
would happen. Perhaps peace could break out. The world might be
menacing because one is shooting at it. The term *vicious cycle* captures the essence of this paradigm. Wachtel (1993) points out the
irony of this cyclical psychodynamic where the individual ends up
recreating the very situation that he or she most fears.

To continue with the war metaphor, I am reminded of a movie
about a sole Japanese soldier who had been defending an island in
the Pacific, not knowing that World War II had been over for many
years. Such is the fate of many of our clients who are anachronisti-

---

[9] It is probably just as valid to say that sometimes therapists are also "stuck," rather than seeing them as inadequate, uneducable, or "bad" clinicians.

cally trapped by a "defense system" that once functioned as a necessary (adaptive) security system but lost its usefulness many years ago.
This idea is also reflected in the perspective of the solution-focused
therapists—that what was once the solution has now become the
problem. The reasons for digging the hole made sense at the time
when one needed protection from unresponsive parents or negative
childhood circumstances, but now that very protection brings about
the conditions one was trying to avoid.

5. **The focus in TLDP is on shifting maladaptive relationship
   patterns and their attendant emotions.**

   The TLDP therapist attends to relational themes in the person's
life, containing emotional and narrative content. (The next chapter
contains a description of how the therapist can discern such interpersonal themes.) From these themes the therapist derives the goals for the
treatment that involve helping the client affectively and cognitively shift
well-established (but dysfunctional) ways of relating to self and other.
(The following section will discuss how to determine these goals.)

   These themes are recognizable in *what* the client says about
his or her previous and current relationships and attitudes toward
oneself and *how* the client interacts in the session. As so much of
what maintains the individual's internal working model is not available for conscious reflection, the client usually cannot directly and/
or coherently discuss it. However, clients cannot help but be who
they are in the interaction with the therapist and will "tell" him or
her through their thoughts, feelings, and actions what is not working in their lives.[10] In deriving such an understanding, the therapist
attends to the client, the interaction with the client, and one's own
emotional experiences.

   From an object relations perspective, the construct of *projective
identification* (Ogden, 1982) is often used to describe a process by
which the therapist comes to feel what the client feels but experiences
the feeling as self-originated (i.e., as one's own feeling). For example,

---

[10]This obvious "telling" reminds me of Edgar Allan Poe's short story "The Purloined Letter," in which a
blackmailer hides a letter containing compromising information in plain sight. So, too, clients reveal their
dysfunctional patterns "in plain sight."

I might start feeling angry as I am sitting with Mr. Johnson. However, TLDP does not assume that Mr. Johnson is "projecting" his unacknowledged anger onto me, only that I am pulled (or pushed) to feel and/or act in a particular way. In some therapeutic situations, the therapist *may* experience within himself or herself what the client is feeling (a sort of interpersonal empathy), but in other cases, the therapist may be having a complementary reaction. Perhaps my frustration is coming from repeated but unsuccessful attempts to get Mr. Johnson to be more collaborative.

What both of these perspectives have in common is that such interactions are seen from a two-person point of view. The client is not merely transferring old feelings and perceptions onto a neutral therapist. Instead the TLDP idea of transference is more transactionally based in the present and therefore leads to very different intervention strategies. Consistent with the relational–interpersonal school, transference is not seen as a distortion, but rather as the client's *plausible perceptions* of the therapist's behavior and intent. In TLDP the therapist is not expected to be a "blank screen" striving for anonymity and avoiding a show of emotion (as if this were possible!).[11] Such a neutral presentation would be quite disastrous from an attachment point of view. All one has to do is watch one of Tronick's videos (Tronick, Als, Adamson, Wise, & Brazelton, 1978) in which he instructs mothers to keep a "still face" in the presence of their infants[12] to see how quickly the children become emotionally dysregulated when deprived of facial responsiveness.

From a TLDP perspective, clients therefore provide invaluable information about their ways of seeing their interpersonal world in the therapy room—both in content (telling their stories) and style (presentation). This is really an ideal situation. Not only will the therapist hear about central themes, he or she will have the opportunity firsthand to get a taste of what it is like to form a relationship with the person in front of them.

---

[11] Actually, Freud (1912/1924) said (in translation) that "the doctor should be opaque to his patients and, like a *mirror*, should show them nothing but what is shown to him" (emphasis added, p. 118).

[12] For an overview of the *still face paradigm*, see Adamson and Frick, 2003.

However, when working with some clients, the therapist's ability to weave flexibly back and forth from a participant to an observer stance (Sullivan, 1953) while remaining emotionally regulated is severely challenged. Such clients have rigid, limited, or extreme interpersonal styles, often coupled with problems in affect regulation. Because these clients, who are often diagnosed with personality disorders, have difficulty experiencing the therapist as a secure base and have a limited interpersonal repertoire, they are more likely to pull for complementary and rewounding reactions from the therapist—what I have termed *interactive countertransference* (Levenson, 1995). As Kiesler (1982, 1988, 1996) would frame it, the therapist inevitably becomes "hooked" into acting out the complementary response to the client's inflexible, maladaptive pattern. From a TLDP point of view, this "hook" is emotional in nature, which makes it especially powerful. As such, these clients end up reenacting with their therapists a transference–countertransference dance that is played out in the sessions.

Mr. Johnson is an example of such a client with a pervasive maladaptive style that pushed and pulled me to respond countertransferentially. (For a contrasting case with a client with less-rigid patterns who was not dysregulating for the therapist, see my work with Ann described in Chapter 4.) Faced with Mr. Johnson's placating style, I found that I was more active than usual. I experienced myself as more reassuring than is typical for me. I came across more like an authority than is my customary manner. And in some instances my frustration with his woe-is-me, pathetic presentation and "yes, but" responses was conveyed by my choice of words and tone of voice.

Even when therapists are trying to appear calm despite being tossed and turned internally, their emotional reactions are often betrayed by verbal and nonverbal cues. Changes in body posture (e.g., a tight, closed, hunched position), facial movements (e.g., a clenched jaw), tone of voice (e.g., harsh and clipped), and the content of interpretations (e.g., belittling comments) can convey the therapists' emotional state. Although I never did act out my fantasy of reaching over and grabbing Mr. Johnson by the lapels and giving him a good shake, there were times (now preserved for posterity on videotape) when there was sarcasm in my voice and my phrasing took a patronizing turn.

For example, at one point, as Mr. Johnson was complaining about how his grown daughter was "off with her other friends, leaving me alone," I commented that "Given all you have done for her, the least she could do is stick around for the rest of your life." It should be noted that my conscious intent here was to be empathic with Mr. Johnson's feelings of loneliness and to promote his feeling the "legitimacy" of his underlying sense of resentment at being abandoned. I felt that I was speaking his inner truth. However, my choice of words and tone of voice conveyed my irritation and frustration. This countertransferential response was not random. It was consistent with what happens when Mr. Johnson interacts with others. My treating Mr. Johnson like he was a recalcitrant child at times was a perfect complement to his helpless, passive, and needy presentation. (And of course, the more domineering and self-assured my manner, the more acquiescent and placating he became.)

The therapists' difficulty in regaining a firm (regulated) footing with such clients makes the work dicey and often leads them to label these clients as "difficult" or even "dreaded." So much of the therapists' energies may need to go toward their own emotional regulation in these cases that they are less available for the therapeutic work at hand. It is critical that therapists eventually regain their sense of equilibrium and help themselves (and their clients) move into a more rewarding way of interacting. (More detail about this "unhooking" process will be provided in the next chapter.)

However, as previously stated, not all clients will act out a dysfunctional dance in the room with the therapist.[13] These clients have more nuanced, flexible, and permeable patterns and can be more self-reflective. They can more easily achieve a platform of trust and safety, a secure base with their therapists from which to examine interpersonal

---

[13] In my previous thinking (Levenson, 1995), I opined that transference–countertransference reenactments were inevitable. I have since changed my mind based on empirical data (e.g., Connolly et al., 1996) and clinical experience.

patterns in the "real world." The focus in these therapies is more often on the clients' relationships with present significant others in their outside lives, whereas the focus for those with more chronic and limited styles needs to also focus on reenactments that are happening in the session. No matter where the client is on this flexible–inflexible continuum, however, the ultimate focus is on relationships with important others and the attachment-based emotions involved.

6. **TLDP is concerned with interactive processes rather than with specific content.**

As is probably evident to the reader by now, TLDP is a process-oriented model—concerned with what goes on within and between people rather than focusing on specific content. No matter what presenting problem or symptom the client brings, the TLDP therapist will be assessing how the individual's issues, even those that get presented as internal struggles (intrapersonal conflict), are a function of repetitive interpersonal cycles maintained by problematic affect or affect regulation difficulties. The approach focuses on patterns and sequences of affectively linked behavior and how each facet of the pattern is dynamically intertwined with the others to cause an overall organizing gestalt. In this way, the person's emotions are both a keyhole into one's compromised attachment system and a key to opening it up. For example, a pivotal session with Mr. Johnson involved his not eating breakfast to get to the session. Focusing on the *process* of how he made the decision not to eat captured essential elements of his lifelong subservient style.

7. **TLDP focuses on one chief problematic relationship pattern.**

While clients may have a repertoire of different interpersonal patterns depending on their states of mind and the particulars of the situation, the emphasis in TLDP is on discerning a client's most pervasive and problematic style of relating. That is not to say that other relationship patterns may not be important. However, focusing on the most frequently troublesome type of interaction should have ramifications for the other less-central interpersonal schemes and is pragmatically essential when time is of the essence. Back to Mr. Johnson. His therapy concentrated on his compliant behavior and concomitant feelings about himself and others. He also had problems with somatization and isolation, but these were not the direct focus of the work. Figuring out what is the chief pattern is based on redundancies of interactive and emotional processes between and within individuals.

8. **The therapist is both a participant and an observer.**

When the therapist is more aware of being in the observing mode, his or her roles can take the form of choreographer, coach, process consultant, guide, cheerleader, and/or teacher, to name a few. In these roles, the therapist can help clients consciously access, label, and come to understand their emotional–interpersonal life through what affective neuroscientists refer to as verbal, explicit, linguistic processes (Schore, 2003a, 2003b, 2006). When the therapist is more immersed in the participant role, he or she is in the trenches with the client. Here the therapist is more aware of himself or herself as his or her own person, rather than being in a helper role. From this perspective, the therapist feels oneself as a sentient human being, albeit with specialized training, who is trying to have a relationship with another. As a participant, the therapist is relating to the client more from an emotionally engaged, non-self-conscious place that can inform the therapist about the client's "unthought known" (Bollas, 1987). Some would refer to as this capacity as the province of the nonconscious, nonverbal, implicit, emotion-processing "right brain" (Schore, 2006). The therapist weaves back and forth from the experience of being more an understanding observer to more an enacting participant— from the explicit to the implicit and from the active to receptive. The observer–participant roles should not be thought of as a dichotomy, or even two ends of the same continuum, but rather as a dialectic of "both/and."[14]

---

[14] Even at those times when the therapist feels himself or herself to be an observer, I agree with Safran and Muran's (2000) argument that the therapist is always, *to some extent,* an unwitting participant whose understanding of what is going on in the therapeutic relationship is partial at best.

9. **The change process will continue after the therapy is terminated.**

The overarching goal in TLDP is to interrupt the client's ingrained, repetitive, dysfunctional cycle that reverberates within and between individuals. While the client may have had some opportunities to take interpersonal risks (inside and outside the therapy room), such changes may be tentative and nascent. It is expected that over time as one has more opportunities to experience healthier behaviors in his or her own life, interactions with others will shift accordingly and become more rewarding. As a result the individual will then have an increased sense of self-efficacy and better emotional regulation, leading to an increased sense of safety and an appraisal that it is safe enough to take yet further risks to connect with others in a more open way. These healthier behaviors implicitly invite others to respond more positively, leading to yet more fruitful interactions with others, a fuller sense of self, and so on. With enough such experiences, these more adaptive, flexible "victorious" cycles come to alter the previously constraining internalized working model. It is a case of what goes around comes around. As I like to say, the therapy sessions end, but the therapeutic work needs to continue for the rest of the person's life in the outside world.

## GOALS

There are two major goals for TLDP: (a) providing *new experiences* for the client (both within oneself and relationally with others) and (b) providing *new understandings* for the client (regarding both emotional shifts within and relational shifts between). These goals (new experiences and understandings) and foci (within and between), however, are not to be seen as dichotomous, separate, reified entities. Rather they are designed to provide therapists with heuristically useful referents guiding them to make conceptually clearer choices with regard to formulation and intervention strategies.

## New Experiences

Experiential learning involves healthier, more functional, relational inter-actions that challenge cyclical maladaptive patterns and promotes a more positive, less defended, expanded sense of self as well as more positive expectations of others. This goal emphasizes the affective and action-oriented component of change: feeling differently (and being aware of feeling differently and the attendant pull to act differently in the process) and also its reverse—acting differently, being aware of acting differently, and feeling differently in the process.

The emphasis on experiential learning has tremendous implications for who is an appropriate client for TLDP. It is not just the introspective, self-reflective, intelligent, and highly verbal person who can benefit. Even those who not psychologically minded and who think in more concrete terms usually know when they have had a new experience. They know when something is happening that is outside their usual frame of reference. They might not be able to conceptualize this new experience fully, or even talk about it, but they usually have a felt sense (Gendlin, 1991) that they are encountering something unexpected and potentially worthwhile. This emphasis on having a new experience as a major goal allows us to accept a much *wider range of clients* into treatment than many other psychodynamic brief therapies that focus on understanding through interpretation.

Another reason for stressing experiential learning is because of the power of such learning to affect change. You do not have to be a clinician very long to encounter clients who can talk knowledgeably, even insight-fully, about their dynamics, especially if they have had multiple, insight-oriented therapies. They can sometimes wax eloquently about their fears of surpassing their fathers, inhibitions about commitment, or even their "Oedipal conflicts." On occasion, they can even provide their DSM-IV diagnoses. But often they are not leading happier, more fulfilled, more rewarding, or more functional lives. The "truth" has not set them free, challenging the pursuit of insight alone as *the* goal.

In an elaboration of my previous conceptualization of "the new experience" (Levenson, 1995), I now perceive that there are *two major types of new experiences*—those focusing on interpersonal experiences and those focusing on internal processes.[15] The first type is one that I have written about previously—the new experience that results when one engages in atypical interpersonal behaviors with others. The second type is focused on internal processes that occur when the client experiences a direct shift in emotion. This internal focus has been influenced by the work of the experiential theorists, emotionally focused therapists, and developmental neuroscientists. From a TLDP perspective, what both of these types of experiential learning have in common is that the therapist encourages any feelings, thoughts, or actions that will disrupt their clients' more typical inflexible, constricted proclivities.

It should be noted that this is not about offering "good enough" generic experiences. A therapist needs to specifically choose from all the respectful and mature ways of intervening, those particular aspects that would most undermine a client's particular dysfunctional style. From a thorough understanding of the client's maladaptive pattern (formulation), the therapist identifies what new experience(s) would most likely subvert the client's maladaptive interactions and self-views.[16] What are needed are *specific, idiosyncratic* goals. The therapist–client "interaction has to be about the right content—a content that we would call insight if it became explicit" (Gill, 1993, p. 115).

### Focus on the Interpersonal

To have a new interpersonal experience, clients must take a step forward (with their therapists and/or others in their lives) in the face of anxiety or some other warded-off feeling state such as shame or helplessness. When clients take a risk in behaving differently, they experience themselves differently both directly through prioprioceptive and emotional channels and indirectly by consciously noticing themselves behaving differently and mentalizing this awareness.

After taking new steps, whether they be in the form of a shift in affective expression (like staring defiantly at another), verbal output (telling

---

[15] However, the reader should understand that even when the therapist is focusing on the client's internal processes, at some basic level this too is a dyadic relational act.

[16] The TLDP method of formulating a case is covered in the next chapter.

someone what one wants), or physical actions (standing in place), the client observes, sometimes with bated breath, how the other person reacts, as manifested in that person's emotional expression, words, and/or deeds. In this way the individual not only has a new experience of self, but also a new experience of the other person and of their joint interaction. These new experiences (especially once they are consciously noticed and appraised) have the opportunity over time to shift the old internal working model. As alternative behaviors occur and are rewarded, new patterns evolve and old patterns are relinquished.

Since the client's original, dysfunctional style was learned interpersonally through a series of antecedents and consequences that become inextricably linked and recursive, a more functional interpersonal style can be learned through a new series of antecedents and consequences. Thus there is an isomorphism between how the dysfunction occurred (interpersonally) and how it can be ameliorated (interpersonally). This affectively linked behavioral learning is a critical component in the practice of TLDP. As Frieda Fromm-Reichman is credited with saying, *what the patient needs is an experience, not an explanation.*

The main reason people do not quickly unlearn patterns that have become maladaptive is that people avoid what they see as the source of their apprehension. This avoidance behavior is reinforced (negatively) because it keeps one's anxiety low. The real danger is that such defensive avoidance becomes chronic and deprives the person of the opportunity to unlearn the mistaken attribution. The child who was bitten by a *particular* dog when young now tries to avoid *all* dogs (sometimes not even consciously aware of why he or she is doing so). Furthermore, the situation becomes even more complex, because when the child is around a dog, he or she behaves in anxious ways that invite more aggressive or other unfriendly canine behavior, reinforcing the child's initial fear. One can readily understand the need for helping the child approach dogs and sustain enough regulation to invite a different, more pleasant response. Thus, quite often from the person's point of view, things often feel worse before they can feel better.

Let's return to Mr. Johnson. Very early in life, his healthy ebullience met with his father's harsh treatment, resulting in Mr. Johnson's fear of his father and leading to his not expressing and eventually not even feeling his core enlivening affects. This fear then generalized to other people, and his avoidance of the anxiety that would reappear if he were more assertive further reinforced Mr. Johnson's placating behaviors (and probably his isolation as well). What would help is Mr. Johnson is having a series of experiences (inside and outside my office) in which he behaves assertively without incurring the retribution he so desperately fears.

There are parallels between this type of experiential learning and procedures used in other types of therapy such as treating affect phobia through exposure (McCullough et al., 2003), experiential disconfirmation (Safran & Segal, 1990), and passing clients' tests (Sampson & Weiss, 1986). Alexander and French's (1946) concept of a corrective emotional experience (covered in the previous chapter) is also applicable.

### Focus on the Intrapersonal

The second type of experiential learning focuses on shifting (i.e., transforming) emotions within the individual directly (i.e., *not* through lessening anxiety by taking interpersonal risks). One way to do this is to *change emotion with emotion* (Greenberg, 2002). "A maladaptive emotional state can be transformed best by 'undoing' it with another more adaptive emotion" (Greenberg & Pascual-Leone, 2006, p. 618). A positive emotional state can be promoted directly. In terms of the client's subjective sense, things do not have to get worse before they get better.

Greenberg and Pascual-Leone (2006) make the apt point that changing emotion with emotion is more than catharsis, exposure, or attenuation. It is actually the introduction of a new (incompatible) feeling that undoes, integrates into, and alters the old feeling. They give an example of how introducing adaptive anger can be used to shift a client's maladaptive fear. "Thus, the action tendency to . . . flee in fear is transformed by the tendency to thrust forward as part of newly accessed anger at violation" (p. 619).

Again, back to Mr. Johnson. In the second session, he was bemoaning the fact that he "had to" loan his adult daughter money that enabled her to be with her "other friends" rather than with him, which left him feeling lonely, depressed, and worthless. While he was experiencing these feelings of powerlessness, I amplified (through validating, heightening, reflecting, and reframing) glimmers of his nascent anger at the way his daughter had treated him in the past. By the end of a 20-session therapy, Mr. Johnson felt entitled to be "righteously angry"; he felt more vitality, and his depression markedly lessened. In addition, his empowered attitude and behavior had interpersonal sequelae—his daughter actually enjoyed being around him more, which is what he wanted in the first place.

Related to the topic of transforming affect directly is the role of experiencing and processing *positive emotions*. The primary focus of psychotherapy has been on reducing or eliminating negative emotions (e.g., depression, anxiety), and there has been scant attention to promoting positive ones. However, empirical findings suggest that positive emotions "broaden one's thought-action repertoire while also 'undoing' the physiological arousal associated with negative emotions and specific action tendencies" (Bridges, 2006, p. 553). They are also adaptive in that they lead to more creative problem solving (Fredrickson, 2001), with resilient people using positive affect to combat negative emotional experiences. This is a different way of thinking about change in therapy and has implications for working briefly and building on the strengths of the individual.[17]

Another way to transform emotions directly is through a *shared implicit relationship* with the therapist—what Stern and the Process of Change Study Group (1998) refer to as "the 'something more' than interpretation" (p. 903). Stemming from work done with caregivers and infants on the developmental process of change, the therapist, like the "good enough" parent, experiences an intersubjective alignment of motives and desires with the client and a mutual, affective attunement achieved through empathic connections, misses, and repairs. Furthermore, the client senses through the therapist's emotionally regulated (and regulating) presence (a gentle tone of voice, a steady gaze) that there is nothing to fear here. It is the mother standing beside the fearful child as an unknown dog approaches—the child glancing at mom (i.e., *reflective appraisal*) to see if there is any reason for concern. It is the child's sense in that moment that the mother understands that he is afraid and that her calmness is a direct message to him.

---

[17] See also a special issue of *Journal of Psychotherapy Integration* (2008) devoted to theory and research on the use of positive emotions in therapy.

Siegel (2006) and others (e.g., Cosolino, 2006; Iacoboni, 2008) writing on neuroscience and interpersonal processes conclude that

> being empathic with patients may be more than just something that helps them 'feel better'; it may create a new state of neural activation . . . that improves the capacity for self-regulation. What is at first a form of interpersonal integration in the sharing of affective and cognitive states now evolves into a form of internal integration in the patient. (Siegel, 2006, p. 255)

This is what is meant by being known in the mind (Fonagy & Target, 2006) and heart (Fosha, 2000) of the other that leads to a sense of safety, security, and dyadically, bidirectionally, regulated positive affective states.[18]

In a similar vein, Fosha (2000) speaks eloquently about the power of core affect to heal in and of itself. "Activating a client's capacity to experience deep affect gives him a taste of what defense-free functioning is like" (p. 271). By using "explicit empathy and radical engagement," Fosha describes how the therapist needs to use vivid, evocative language and speak in short sentences to help clients embrace and deepen their affect throughout the therapy. Similarly, Johnson (2004) enumerates ways the therapist can help clients more fully experience their primary emotions (e.g., by slowing the pace, speaking softly, using images). It is no coincidence that both Fosha (2000, p. 272) and Johnson (2004, p. 109), who are proponents of short-term work, speak of "holding" a client with the quality of the voice, eye contact, and even touch.

## New Understandings

The second TLDP goal of providing a new understanding pertains to helping clients *reflect on and make meaning* of their emotional and relational experiences. This goal focuses more on using one's ability to symbolize experience through language. Like experiential processing, in

---

[18]There is some basic research in the area of neuronal structures and processes (e.g., mirror neuron system) that suggests that we have the capacity for experiencing and representing the intentions of someone else's mind (Gallese, 2003), leading to speculations that this may be the root of empathy.

TLDP, cognitive processing goes on from two perspectives—one more intrapersonal and one more interpersonal.

### Focus on the Intrapersonal

From the intrapersonal perspective, the therapist stays very close to *moment-to-moment feeling states* that are being evoked and expressed in sessions and fosters the client's understanding of the relevancy and meaning of these emotional experiences. For example, Mr. Johnson and I came to understand that he had avoided being in touch with his anger toward his daughter because he feared that such anger would be an indication he was "selfish." With such an understanding, clients can reflect on their heretofore unacknowledged or misunderstood emotional experiences to make meaning where none previously existed and/or to recast old meanings into a more fruitful, more fully coherent narratives.

From a truly interpersonal perspective, the therapist is also tuning into his or her own moment-to-moment feelings and reflecting on these as a reading of his or her interactive countertransference—a snapshot of what it is like to be in relationship with the client in that moment. Cognitively processing these transactional reactions not only enables the therapist to reregulate his or her own arousal (when necessary), but also may inform the therapist's working formulation of the client's dysfunctional maladaptive pattern. As part of an inductive–deductive mutual feedback loop system, the formulation, in turn, provides a coherent narrative that helps the therapist recognize relevant affect states in self and client as they are occurring.

### Focus on the Interpersonal

The goal here is to help clients identify, comprehend, and understand their *interactive patterns* and the reasons for developing and maintaining them. To accomplish these, the therapist might use common psychotherapeutic techniques such as reflection, interpretation, clarification, confrontation, and talking about any patterns emerging between client and therapist. To facilitate a new interpersonal understanding, the TLDP therapist can highlight repetitive patterns that have emerged with the therapist, with past significant others, and with present significant others, as well as those patterns involving how one treats one's self.

Clients begin to recognize their own patterns when they see how similar interpersonal processes occur with different people in their lives. In fact, I often have clients do "homework" where they practice seeing particular dynamics reoccurring with significant others in their daily lives. This new perspective enables them to examine their active role in perpetuating dysfunctional interactions with others and promotes self-observation. Once clients can recognize dysfunctional patterns and connect them to their own feelings, they can then focus on becoming aware in the moment of when such dysfunctional interactions are about to occur. This growing sensitivity enables the client to see and even anticipate opportunities to do something differently.[19]

As the therapist helps clients delineate their interactive patterns, he or she also works with clients to appreciate how the idea of "blame" does not make much sense from this perspective. It is not that someone casts the first stone and therefore is the perpetrator with the other the resultant victim. Rather *all* parties are caught up in a dynamic that sweeps them into acting and reacting, thereby confirming their worst fears and expectations. I very much like how Sue Johnson (2004) in her emotionally focused couples therapy approach helps couples see how the interactive cycle they get into is "the enemy," not their partners. This is similar to the concept of "externalization" as used in narrative therapy (White & Epston, 1990).

In the case of Mr. Johnson, he began to understand how his wife interpreted his passivity as disinterest in her. And he could see how her "demanding" behavior was really her attempt to get him to stay close to her. He came to appreciate that they were both caught up in a dysfunctional, interpersonal, maladaptive cycle.

Not only does TLDP encourage a nonblaming stance with others, it also takes a nonblaming stance toward the self—promoting self-compassion and thereby lessening the client's shame and/or guilt. The therapist can help depathologize clients' behavior and emotional reactions by helping them understand their historical development. From the TLDP point of

---

[19] Binder (2004) using a concept from Schon (1983) refers to this ability as "reflection-in-action," which is defined as the process of appraising and modifying one's own behavior in real time so as to be able to shift the behavior while it is occurring. Although Binder used it referring to a therapist competency, this capacity is important for clients as well.

view, feelings and dysfunctional behaviors are the individual's attempt to adapt to threatening situations when safe and secure attachments are not possible. For example, in therapy Mr. Johnson began to understand that as a child he had to be subservient and hypervigilant in order to avoid beatings and still maintain the thread of a connection to his parents. He came to see how his meek stance and withdrawn behavior were really his best efforts to "keep the peace." This realization enabled him to view his present interpersonal style from a different perspective and allowed him to have some empathy for his childhood plight.

The therapist's observations about the reenactments of the cyclical maladaptive pattern in the sessions (including the therapist's self-disclosure of how he or she feels pushed and pulled in the interaction) provide a potentially potent in vivo learning opportunity. By ascertaining how the pattern has emerged in the therapeutic relationship, the client has, perhaps for the first time, the opportunity to examine the nature of those behaviors that make up the pattern in a relatively safe environment. Therapist and client can step back from the heat of the interaction and metacommunicate about what has just transpired—what has been co-created and re-created—between them.

Of course, the degree to which clients can comprehend, generalize, and expand on any new understanding is limited by such factors as their intellectual abilities, capacity for introspection, and psychological mindedness.[20] For some concrete-thinking clients, perhaps the most they can understand is a linear connection between their behavior and another's response. Others with more psychological sophistication can appreciate the nuances of their interactive patterns, can delineate how their patterns of relating began, and can discern the subtle manner in which they might be manifested in the present.

---

[20] Relevant research from attachment theory reminds us, however, that one's capacity for psychological mindedness or mentalization can be affected by the degree to which one is exposed to coherent narratives (e.g., Fonagy & Target, 2006). Thus, one cannot overlook the possibility that understanding and appreciating one's patterns in a coherent way could foster such psychological mindedness, thereby taking what has been seen as a precondition for brief therapy and making it an outcome.

## A RAPPROCHEMENT

Although I have made a distinction between new experiences and new understandings, in "real life" they are all part of an interlocking whole. That is, new experiences involve cognitive representations, and new understandings (if they are to be more than intellectualizations) have affective components. I present them here as distinct concepts to help those learning the model be more precise in choosing their interventions. In addition, I have found that psychodynamically oriented therapists have been so trained to intervene with interpretations that highlighting the importance of a *new relational experience* helps remind them that (to paraphrase an old maxim), "an experience is worth a thousand words." Experiential clinicians (e.g., Greenberg & Paivio, 1997), psychodynamic theoreticians (e.g., Fonagy & Target, 2006), interpersonal neurobiologists (e.g., Siegel, 2006), affective neuroscientists (e.g., Panksepp, 1998), and developmental researchers (e.g., Hesse, Main, Abrams, & Rifkin, 2003) all agree that interweaving back and forth between some form of experiential and cognitive learning serves an integrative function leading to healthier personal and interpersonal functioning.

In the next chapter I will discuss the process of putting the theory into practice.

# The Therapy Process

In this chapter, ways to formulate and intervene in time-limited dynamic psychotherapy (TLDP) are presented. In addition, I provide a detailed case to illustrate.

## FORMULATION: THE CYCLICAL MALADAPTIVE PATTERN

In the past, psychodynamic brief therapists used their intuition, expertise, and clinical experience to devise formulations of cases. While these methods worked wonderfully for the gifted clinician, they were impossible to teach explicitly and research programmatically. One remedy for this situation was the development of a procedure for deriving a dynamic focus in TLDP—the cyclical maladaptive pattern (CMP) (Schacht, Binder, & Strupp, 1984). The CMP describes the cycles or patterns people get into that involve inflexible, self-perpetuating behaviors, self-defeating expectations, and negative self-appraisals and that lead to dysfunctional and maladaptive interactions with others (Butler & Binder, 1987; Butler, Strupp, & Binder, 1993).

The CMP provides an organizational framework that makes comprehensible a large mass of data and leads to fruitful hypotheses. In keeping with other modern brief dynamic psychotherapies, this way of formulating is not seen as an encapsulated version of "truth," but rather as a *plausible narrative*, incorporating major components of a person's current and historical interactive world. As Strupp and Binder (1984) have framed it, it is a map of the territory—not the territory itself. A TLDP formulation should provide a blueprint for the entire therapy. It should describe the nature of the intrapersonal and interpersonal dynamics, lead to the delineation of goals, suggest where the client (and the therapist) may become emotionally dysregulated, guide particular interventions, enable the therapist to anticipate in and out of session reenactments, and provide a way to assess whether the therapy is on the right track—in terms of outcome at termination as well as in-session mini-outcomes. Thus, the CMP way of focusing is integrally tied to the therapeutic process. By helping the therapist to intervene in ways that are relevant for the goals for treatment, the therapy can be time-efficient and effective at the same time.

The timing of when to formulate a case is a dilemma for the brief therapist. If one does not formulate early enough, the therapy will be half over before one knows how to intervene. (Remember my experience in my internship with 3-month evaluations?) If one formulates too quickly, the therapist may proceed down a wrong or secondary path. In general, the more repetition one can see in a variety of emotional-relationship patterns, the more confident one can be in formulating early. It is, therefore, easier to formulate the presentation of individuals with limited and rigid styles. Their behavior is often so stereotypical that dysfunctional themes are more readily discernible in their narratives and interactions with others (including in-session transference–countertransference reenactments). Dysfunctional interactional patterns that are more subtle or that depend on a particular state or situation to emerge are more difficult to formulate (but, then again, usually easier to treat). The best advice is to think of the *CMP as a fluid, individualistic, working formulation that is meant to be refined* throughout the therapy.

## CMP Categories

The CMP is comprised of four categories around which a thematic narrative is developed. In my latest thinking, I see that the dysfunctional cycles are held together by and permeated with affect—that emotional processes make up the underlying fabric of the CMP and serve an organizing and directing function for the internalized working model. This is in keeping with the stance that "emotion is not just affect, but a dynamic network of thoughts, feelings, motives, expectations, and sensory and bodily experience" (Greenberg & Paivio, 1997, p. 3).

1. *Acts of the Self.*[1] These include the thoughts, feelings, motives, percep-tions, and behaviors of the client of an interpersonal nature. For example, "When I meet strangers, I believe they are out for their own self-interest" (thought). "I am afraid to go to the dance" (feeling). "I wish I were the life of the party" (motive). "It seemed she was on my side" (perception). "I start crying when I get angry with my husband" (behavior). Sometimes these acts are conscious as those above, and sometimes they are outside awareness. Of particular relevance are those emotions that are disowned or distorted and their attendant attachment needs.

2. *Expectations of Others' Reactions.* This category pertains to all the statements having to do with how the individual imagines others will react to him or her. "My boss will fire me if I make a mistake." "If I go to the dance, no one will ask me to dance." A large part of one's expectations is made up of the emotional valence with which he or she holds that expectation. Often these expectations reveal the person's deep-seated attachment fears, what is being avoided and why.

3. *Acts of Others Toward the Self.* This third grouping consists of the behaviors of other people, as observed (or assumed) and interpreted by the client. "When I made a mistake at work, my boss shunned me for the rest of the day." "When I went to the dance, guys asked me to dance, but only because they felt sorry for me." The perceived acts of others often give the rationale for the person's actions and related affects.

4. *Acts of the Self Toward the Self (Introject).* In this section belong all of the client's behaviors, feelings, or thoughts concerning oneself—when

---

[1] Strupp and Binder (1984) emphasized action (i.e., "acts") in each of the four components of the CMP because they wanted to move away from formulations using static traits (e.g., introverted, grandiose) or theoretical abstractions (e.g., repressed orality). Furthermore, they felt the therapist's empathy might be more easily evoked by an action's concreteness, because he or she might recall having acted in a similar manner. This emphasis on "acts" is consistent with an emotional focus where one of the functions of emotions is to elicit *action* tendencies.

the self is the object. How do clients treat themselves? "When no one asked me to dance, I told myself it's because I'm fat, ugly and unlovable, and poured myself a drink." Quite often the person's introject revolves around acts of self-condemnation and feelings of inadequacy and downright worthlessness. The example above is where the individual was conscious of these feelings and could voice them. But so often people are unaware of the negative messages they are sending themselves. These messages, however, become obvious ("hidden in plain sight") through, for example, the words clients use (e.g., "I *should have* . . ."), voice quality (e.g., mocking), posture (e.g., slumped), and visceral changes (e.g., upset stomach). Here, too, the therapist must be ever vigilant for subtle shifts in the person's behavior that might lead to understanding the emotional underpinnings of that person's introject.

When I am giving TLDP workshops, I like showing a *New Yorker* cartoon that captures the essence of the external–internal interplay of treatment by others and view of self (introject). The cartoon depicts a dog standing amid shreds of paper with a telltale bit of paper in his mouth looking at himself and the destruction he has caused in a mirror. The dog is saying to his reflection, "Bad dog!"[2]

5. *Therapist's Interactive Countertransference.* In addition to the four categories of the CMP, I have added a fifth category—the therapist's interactive countertransference. What are your reactions to the client? What are you pulled to do or not do? What is happening in your gut, in your mind, in your heart? Especially with the "difficult" client who has a more rigid style, the therapist's internal and external responses can provide important sources of information for understanding the person's lifelong dysfunctional interactive pattern. One's reactions to the client usually make sense given the client's interpersonal pattern.[3] Of course, each therapist has a unique personality that might contribute to the particular shading of the

---

[2] Over 100 years ago, the sociologist Cooley (1902) termed these reflected self-appraisals "the looking glass self."

[3] Ivy (2006) writing on the characteristics of a good formulation, uses my (Levenson, 1995) version of the CMP as a case example. He opines that the steps in the formulation process are spelled out and that the theoretical model is straightforward and jargon-free. He particularly notes that "its inclusion of the therapist's emotional responsiveness to the patient as a source of formulation information" (p. 325) distinguishes it from earlier psychodynamic formulation models that assume a detached and neutral therapist.

reaction that is elicited by the client, but the assumption from a TLDP perspective is that the therapist's behavior is *predominantly* shaped by the client's evoking patterns.[4]

## Steps in Case Formulation

Table 4.1 presents the three major tasks involved in deriving a TLDP formulation: assessment, conceptualization, and treatment planning.

| Table 4.1    Steps in TLDP Formulation |
| --- |

### Assessment

The therapist:

1. Lets the client tell his or her own story in his or her own words and manner.
2. Conducts an anchored history.
3. Attends to the emotional flavor of the story (including nonverbal signs).
4. Explores the emotional–interpersonal context related to symptoms or problems.
5. Uses the categories of the CMP to gather, organize, and probe for information.

### Conceptualization

6. Listens for themes in the client's transactional behaviors and concomitant emotions (in past and present relationships as well as with the therapist).
7. Is aware of his or her reciprocal behavioral and emotional reactions (countertransferential pushes and pulls).
8. Is vigilant for reenactments of dysfunction interactions in the therapeutic relationship.
9. Develops a CMP narrative (story) describing the client's predominant dysfunctional emotional–interactive pattern.

### Treatment Planning

10. Uses the CMP to formulate what new experiences (intrapersonally and interpersonally) might lead to more adaptive relating (Goal 1).
11. Uses the CMP to formulate what new understandings (intrapersonally and interpersonally) might lead to more adaptive relating (Goal 2).
12. Revises and refines the CMP throughout therapy.
13. For each of the foregoing steps, considers the influence of cultural factors.

---

[4]This is not to say that there are not times when the therapist's own personality and/or idiosyncratic issues interfere with the therapy. This has been called *classic countertransference* (Gelso, 2004). In these cases consultation, supervision, and/or one's own therapy are necessary to limit any untoward impact on the therapy. On the other hand, interactive countertransference is thought of as a more universal reaction to the client's style and very useful in understanding the client's dynamics.

Subsumed under these tasks are 13 steps useful in formulating a case. These steps should not be thought of as separate procedures applied in a linear, rigid fashion, but rather as guidelines for the therapist to be used in a fluid manner (Levenson & Strupp, 1999).

### Assessment

To derive a TLDP formulation, the therapist lets the client tell his or her own story (**Step 1**) in the initial sessions rather than relying on the traditional psychiatric interview to gather specific information about developmental history, educational background, etc. By listening to *how* the client tells his or her story (e.g., deferentially, cautiously, dramatically), *what* is included (e.g., lots of information about how he or she is in distress), and what is left out (e.g., no comment on other people), the therapist can learn much about the client's interpersonal style. In responding to the client in these initial sessions, the therapist expands the client's story by conducting an "anchored history" (**Step 2**) in which he or she starts with where the client is and then asks questions that are designed to help the client and therapist understand what led up to particular actions, feelings, and attributions. For example, when Mr. Johnson said he started drinking when his daughter didn't visit, I inquired about other times when he felt ignored or abandoned.

In particular, the therapist attends to the emotional flavor of the client's narrative (**Step 3**). Are there signs of emotional overstimulation (e.g., forgetting what one was talking about, holding the arms of the chair for dear life, uncontrolled laughter)? Are there signs of dampened emotionality (dry rendition of the "facts," blank facial expression, stiff body position)? The emotions and feelings the person expresses during his or her story will often be bookmarks to those parts that are particularly relevant.

The therapist then explores the interpersonal–emotional context of the client's symptoms or problems (**Step 4**). When did the problems begin? What else was going on in the client's life at that time, especially of an interpersonal nature? In conjunction with this exploration into relational dynamics, the therapist begins to explore the intrapersonal dynamics. Where is the person's pain? What parts of themselves have clients had to disown, tone down, or distort to make themselves acceptable to others?

The therapist uses the categories of the CMP to suggest areas where additional information is needed (**Step 5**). For example, does the therapist know a great deal about how other people have treated the client (acts of others), but almost nothing about how the client treats himself or herself (acts of self toward self)? I have found that actually writing down the information organized by the CMP categories can be helpful for tracking changes over time and developing the client's interpersonal story. A schematic form for doing so is provided in Figure 4.1.

| Figure 4.1  Form for the Cyclical Maladaptive Pattern (CMP) | |
|---|---|
| **Identifying Information:** | |
| Acts of the Self | |
| Expectations of Others' Behaviors | |
| Acts of Others | |
| Acts of Self Toward Self | |
| Countertransference Reactions | |
| **Goals:** | |
| New Experience<br>Intrapersonal:<br><br>Interpersonal: | |
| New Understanding<br>Intrapersonal:<br><br>Interpersonal: | |

Adapted from *Time-Limited Dynamic Psychotherapy: A Guide to Clinical Practice*, by H. Levenson, 1995, and reprinted here with permission of Basic Books, a member of the Perseus Book Group.

## *Conceptualization*

For **Step 6**, the therapist listens for themes in the emerging material linking the four components together. By being sensitive to commonalities and redundancies in the client's transactional and emotional patterns over person, time, and place, the therapist begins to discern a pattern.

Throughout the sessions, the therapist should have a hovering awareness of how he or she feels during the session, especially when pushed or pulled (i.e., interactive countertransference) to respond in a certain way in keeping with the client's expectation of others and/or acts of others (**Step 7**). These pulls are often experienced as visceral changes (e.g., therapist's heart rate increases as client glowers), a change in attention (e.g., therapist begins thinking of how much time is left in the session), affective shifts (e.g., therapist feels like he or she is walking on eggshells), and vivid imagery (e.g., a puppy wagging his tail).

Such self-awareness is of critical importance in TLDP, and there is no easy way to get there. One's own personal therapy, self-reflection, and good supervision/consultation have all been recommended in the psychotherapy literature (see Boswell & Castonguay, 2007). In addition, recently there has been an increased exploration of mindfulness exercises as a way to help therapists recognize and appreciate the significance of their own experience. As observed by Safran and Muran (2000), "gradually, over time, this type of mindfulness work helps trainees to become more aware of subtle feelings, thoughts, and fantasies emerging on the edge of awareness when working with their patients, which can subsequently provide an important source of information about what is occurring in the relationship" (p. 210).

Furthermore, the TLDP formulation method using the CMP is another way therapists can tune into their feelings in session. Through learning how the client has pushed and pulled others to behave in certain ways, the saliency of such behaviors is highlighted, giving the therapist a "heads up" about likely ways he or she will be reacting.

These reactions may result in the therapist's being pulled into responding in a complementary fashion—recruited into becoming an unsuspecting "accomplice" (Kiesler, 1982) in a dysfunctional relational dynamic (**Step 8**). This is not considered to be a "mistake" in TLDP, but rather a reenactment in the here-and-now of the sessions that could be helpful eventually in providing opportunities for experiential learning and cognitive understanding.

In training hundreds of students, I have found the use of videotape invaluable. Prior to coming to supervision, I have students watch videotapes of their sessions. Quite frequently students, now in a very different (more regulated) emotional state, can observe interactions with their clients on tape at a later time and place, and recognize how they are responding in ways that are atypical for them. They can begin to see reenactments unfolding.

By using the four categories of the CMP, the therapist's own reactions to the developing relationship with the client, and any reenactments in the session, the therapist discerns a narrative story that describes the client's predominant dysfunctional emotional–interactive pattern emanating from attachment needs and strivings (**Step 9**). This narrative fits the following outline: The client behaves, feels, and thinks in certain ways regarding transactions with others and has come to expect others to behave in certain ways in response. These expectations are communicated to others primarily through nonverbal, emotional signals that trigger others to behave in ways the client unconsciously expects. The client then reads these complementary behaviors also through an emotional lens, and these apperceptions affect the client's self-appraisal and treatment of himself or herself, which further encourages the client to behave, feel, and think in certain ways, completing the cycle.

### Treatment Planning

From the CMP formulation, the therapist then ascertains the two broad goals for treatment. The first goal involves determining the nature of the new experience (**Step 10**) for this particular client. The therapist discerns what he or she could say or do to help this person have (a) a set of new, relevant, intrapersonal–affective experiences and (b) a set of new, relevant, interpersonal experiences (with the therapist and/or with others) that would most likely subvert or interrupt the client's maladaptive, vicious cycle. After determining the nature of these new experiences, the therapist can use the CMP formulation to determine the second broad goal for treatment—the new understanding (**Step 11**). The therapist figures out how he or she could help the person understand (a) the relevancy and meaning of one's own emotions and (b) the role he or she plays in co-creating a dysfunctional pattern with significant others.

**Step 12** in the formulation process involves the continuous refinement of the CMP throughout the therapy. In a brief therapy, the therapist cannot wait to have all the "facts" before formulating the case and intervening. As the therapy proceeds, new content and interactional data become available and are used to strengthen or alter the working formulation. Thus, the information gleaned from the CMP is invaluable: It guides the therapist in how to handle therapeutic situations to maximize clinical outcome and process—*a necessity when time is of the essence.*

With regard to formulating the case of Mr. Johnson, I could see by the end of the first session that Mr. Johnson was a very passive man, an adaptation he began to make as a child in order to deal with his father's physical and emotional abuse. As an adult, he understandably feared that if he expressed any anger, others would reject or hurt him. Since rejection would be devastating for Mr. Johnson, he learned to be placating—swallowing his anger instead of expressing it. Others unfortunately took advantage of Mr. Johnson's deferential attitude and experienced his sad-sack, passive style as off-putting, leading them to avoid and even reject him. This left Mr. Johnson's feeling worthless and helpless, causing him to be more hopeless and passive, thereby perpetuating the cycle. My experiential goal for Mr. Johnson was to help him recognize his more empowering emotions (e.g., anger) and to help him take some active control over his life. My goal was also to help him understand his own role in fostering the very response he wished to avoid and how his own core feelings could be used to steer him in a more rewarding direction.

The final step (**Step 13**) involves taking into consideration cultural aspects involved in TLDP formulation. *This cultural perspective is one that should permeate all the others.* The therapist needs to be culturally sensitive within each of the formulation steps. The multicultural aspects are so important in formulating and intervening in TLDP that a separate section below is provided.

## Multicultural Aspects

Culture is shared learned behavior that is transmitted from one generation to another for purposes of human adjustment, adaptation,
and growth. Culture has both internal and external referents. External
referents include artifacts, roles, and institutions. Internal referents
include attitudes, values, beliefs, expectations, epistemologies, and
consciousness. (Marsella & Kameoka, 1989, p. 233)

Since TLDP acknowledges that both therapist and client bring their
own personal qualities, history, and values to the therapeutic encounter,
it can be sensitive to all the factors that are involved in making up one's
worldview (e.g., internalized working models). For understanding the
clients' CMPs, consideration of gender, race, ethnicity, sexual orientation,
socioeconomic status, age, disability status, and so on all potentially play a
significant role. The TLDP therapist needs explicitly to consider the larger
context in which any therapy takes place. For example, "it seems crucial
to extend . . . [the notion] of transference to include the organizing
principles and imagery crystallized out of the values, roles, beliefs, and
history of the *cultural* environment" (LaRoche, 1999, p. 391, emphasis
added). Thus, it is of paramount importance that the therapist be aware of
and understand how cultural and worldview factors may be playing a role
in the client's lifelong patterns and in interpersonal difficulties, including
those that might manifest between therapist and client.

From a relational point of view, the client's interpersonal style inside
and outside of the therapy office is an amalgamation of his or her unique
adaptations within a sociocultural context. Given the impact of culture
on one's assumptive world, it would be expected that individuals from a
similar background might manifest some analogous actions, thoughts,
assumptions, and expectations, *and* invite back from people reactions
based on these cultural, racial, personal, and demographic variables.[5]
For example, in our racist society, it is likely that an African-American

---

[5] Of course clients will vary to the degree to which they identify with or adhere to their particular
culture's mores and expectations, and to the degree to which they are acculturated into another (usually
dominant) culture.

child gets treated differently by white teachers (e.g., less positive academic attention) that in turn plays a role in lowering the child's self-esteem and future academic performance. If a therapist does not consider these factors and the role they play in fostering certain cyclical dynamic patterns, important dimensions could be missed or misunderstood, thereby endangering the entire therapeutic process and outcome. Thus, the TLDP therapist must adopt the point of view that cultural parameters and interpersonal working models are inextricably linked.

As part of this understanding, the therapist should have some comprehension (based on the available clinical and empirical data in the literature) of normative interpersonal and intrapersonal behavior and expectations for people who come from the same culture or region, or who share certain physical and/or personal attributes. Obtaining appropriate consultation (or even referring to someone else) is mandatory when cultural knowledge is insufficient. Of course, clients can also provide invaluable information regarding the ways and extent to which culture plays a role. They may not be able to say directly, but asking exploratory questions such as the following can be helpful: "Would others [from your culture] interpret this as you do? Would others [from your culture] understand what you are going through? Would others be responding as you are responding to this situation?" Do clients perceive that their feelings, attitudes, and/or behaviors are alienating them from others with whom they usually identify?

To illustrate, with a case of a trainee (Levenson, 1995), Mrs. Follette was a divorced, 59-year-old, African-American woman who worked as an office administrator. She complained of feeling inferior and said other people kept her at arm's length. Is this to be understood as part of her idiosyncratic CMP or as part of set of experiences she shares with other women of color, women of a "certain age," and people holding certain jobs in our society? And if it is shared by others with a similar cultural background, how is her manifestation of it unique? In this particular case, the client described how she longed for closeness with her *female relatives* and felt different from them in her ability to achieve this intimacy. Thus, the therapist hypothesized that her presenting complaints were more informative of her idiosyncratic (unique) adaptations, rather than those she held in common with other women, other African Americans, and other people of that socioeconomic status.[6]

But taking into account the client's culture is only one of four perspectives relevant to obtaining a culturally sensitive TLDP formulation. Another perspective involves the therapists' taking into consideration how their working models have been influenced by *their own culture* in which they were raised, live, and/or use as a reference group. Does the therapist understand the cultural lens through which he or she sees the world?

The third perspective focuses on how the entire therapeutic endeavor has its own culture with proscribed roles, expectations, beliefs, and institutions.[7] For example, in our society, there is an inherent power differential between the therapist and the client. The last perspective concerns how all of these might interact. How might the worldview of the client and that of the therapist dynamically relate within the frame of a therapy?

In Mrs. Follette's case, the therapist was a single, Caucasian, third-year psychiatry resident, young enough to be the client's son. The client and therapist differed with regard to marital status, race, gender, ethnicity, socioeconomic status, and age, to name a few. How might these differences play out in the sessions? Perhaps this client reported being held at arm's length because of experiences she was having (or expectations she might be holding) working with a white male—a *cultural* transference–countertransference reenactment (i.e., stemming from institutionalized racism and sexism). If this were the case, her therapist could make a serious error by inferring that this was solely a personal issue for her. From a TLDP perspective, it is important to be aware of the dangers of making assumptions based solely on transference–countertransference enactments. This again highlights the importance of a comprehensive and evolving formulation using the CMP categories and information about relevant multicultural factors pertinent to the client, therapist, setting, and their interaction.

---

[6] Ridley and Kelly (2007) outline nine useful micro-decisions to help the therapist discern which data are more cultural and which are more idiosyncratic.

[7] For a thoughtful (and thought-provoking) view of this perspective, the reader is referred to Jerome Frank's 1961 classic book on *Persuasion and Healing*, now in its third edition (Frank & Frank, 1991).

## INTERVENTION STRATEGIES

Implementation of TLDP does not rely on a set of techniques. Rather, interventions in TLDP are seen as therapeutic *strategies* that are inextricably embedded in an interpersonal relationship. Therefore, all TLDP interventions are considered to be relational acts (Norcross, 2002)—even those that seem rather concrete and straightforward like assigning homework. As Butler and Strupp (1986) concluded, interventions "cannot be reduced to a set of disembodied techniques because techniques gain their meaning and, in turn, their effectiveness from the particular interaction of the individuals involved" (p. 33).

In theory, any intervention that could facilitate the goals of new experiencing and new understanding can be used in TLDP. In my work with clients, I feel free to use whatever strategies are within my therapeutic armamentarium. In addition to traditional psychodynamic interventions (e.g., clarification, confrontation, interpretation), I have used the gestalt empty-chair technique, bodily focusing, mindful meditation, metaphor/ storytelling, behavioral rehearsal, psychoeducation, reframing, analysis of dreams, suggestion, and homework, to name a few. Given the brevity of the work, clients become accustomed to brief therapists using a variety of pragmatically designed strategies. Furthermore, as the interventions are all designed to promote the same major goals, they have a common, coherent theme. Phenomenologically, they make sense.[8] Also, as stated in the introductory chapter, in brief therapies, therapists are more directive, active, and pragmatic (Levenson, Butler, Powers, & Beitman, 2002). They are more willing and (one hopes) more able to incorporate a variety of potentially useful strategies in a practically helpful way.

Before getting into some of the categories of TLDP interventions, let me make a general comment about when and how to intervene. In brief dynamic therapy, therapists must become comfortable with intervening before they have sufficient information. Often putting forth statements as tentative ("I may have this wrong, but . . .") and seeking feedback from clients ("Do I have that right?"), builds a sense of collaboration and dissuades clients

---

[8] However, it is essential for the therapist to appreciate how the meaning and impact of any intervention shift when it is taken out of its original "home base" theory and incorporated into another model (Messer, 1992).

from believing their therapists are reading their minds and making veridical pronouncements. Interventions do not need to be "correct" in an absolute sense. They can be thought of as invitations to see and feel things in a different way and from a different perspective. Staying close to what is observable and asking for as much detail as possible promotes reflection on the part of the client rather than submissive acceptance (or outright refutation) of what the therapist is saying. ("When I commented on your lateness, I noticed you began looking at the floor and started to talk in a soft voice about how you never get it right. Could we replay this in slow motion—from my comment to your self-condemnation—to see what just happened here between us?")

In my attempt to assimilate attachment theory and emotion-focused experiential approaches into interpersonal therapy, I have taken previously identified TLDP strategies from the Vanderbilt Therapeutic Strategies Scale[9] (VTSS; Butler et al., 1986) and modified them to be more attachment- and affect-based.[10] These 25 strategies are grouped into seven categories described below. (See Table 4.2 for a listing of these items.)

## Maintaining the Therapeutic Relationship

In TLDP, as with most clinical approaches, managing the therapeutic relationship is a critical competency (Binder, 2004). To strengthen the therapeutic alliance, the TLDP therapist engages clients from a respectful and nonjudgmental stance, validates their feelings and perceptions, and invites their collaboration in the process (**Strategy 1**).

It is critical in this relationally based approach that the therapist shows evidence of listening receptively to what the client is saying. This receptivity may be communicated by body position, facial expression, and head nodding (**Strategy 2**). Many of these are culturally determined. In a brief

---

[9] The VTSS was designed by members of the Center for Psychotherapy Research Team at Vanderbilt University as a measure of adherence to TLDP modes of intervention. It is comprised of 12 items concerning general psychodynamic interviewing style and 10 items focused on strategies specific to TLDP. Research indicates that the VTSS is able to reflect changes in therapists' behaviors following training in TLDP (Butler et al., 1987; Butler & Strupp, 1989; Henry et al., 1993b). For a copy of the VTSS with scoring instructions, see Appendix A in Levenson (1995).

[10] While most of the interventions reflected in these items have strong empirical support from both experiential (e.g., Elliott, 2001) and interpersonal fields (e.g., Kiesler, 1996), this modified view of TLDP combining both approaches has not yet been explored in clinical trials. Hopefully, the clinical and theoretical model put forth here can serve as a guide for future empirical investigation.

## Table 4.2    TLDP Strategies

### Maintaining the Therapeutic Relationship

The therapist:

1. Responds to the client conveying a respectful, collaborative, empathic, validating, nonjudgmental stance. (VTSS 4, 5)*

2. Shows evidence of listening receptively. (VTSS 10)

3. Recognizes the client's strengths and conveys this to the client.

4. Addresses obstacles (e.g., silences, coming late, avoidance of meaningful topics) and opportunities (e.g., inquisitiveness, assertiveness, willingness to be vulnerable) that might influence the therapeutic process. (VTSS 20)

### Accessing and Processing Emotion

5. Helps the client stay emotionally regulated.

6. Encourages the client to experience and express affect in the session. (VTSS 1)

7. Facilitates the client's awareness of emotions, and uses various strategies to help deepen his or her emotional experience.

8. Helps the client label emotional experience and recognize its goal-directed significance.

9. Helps the client access, experience, and deepen attachment-related feelings and/or primary emotions specifically related to the CMP.

### Empathic Exploration

10. Uses open-ended questions. (VTSS 12)

11. Inquires into the personal or unique meanings of the client's words. (VTSS 7)

12. Responds to the client's statements or descriptions by seeking concrete detail. (VTSS 8)

### Focused Inquiry

13. Throughout the therapy, maintains a focused line of inquiry. (VTSS 6)

### Relationship Focus

14. Facilitates the client's expression and exploration of feelings, thoughts, and beliefs in relation to significant others (including the therapist or the therapeutic relationship). (VTSS 2, 3, 14)

15. Encourages the client to discuss how the therapist might feel or think about the client. (VTSS 15)

16. Discloses one's own reactions to some aspect of the client's behavior in general and to the client's CMP in particular. (VTSS 16)

17. Metacommunicates about the interpersonal process that is evolving between therapist and client. (VTSS 11, 13, 19)

| Table 4.2   TLDP Strategies *(continued)* |
|---|

### Cyclical Patterns

18. Asks about the client's introject. (VTSS 18)

19. Helps the client link his or her emotions and personal meanings to a recurrent pattern of interpersonal behavior.

20. Deepens the client's emotional and conceptual understanding of how the CMP has affected one's intrapersonal and interpersonal functioning.

21. Links the need for disowning primary emotions to the client's early experiences with caregivers.

22. Helps the client incorporate his or her more adaptive (healthier) feelings, thoughts, and behaviors into a new narrative.

### Promoting Change Directly

23. Provides opportunities for the client to have new experiences of himself or herself in interaction with the therapist and to have new relational experiences in interaction with the therapist in accord with the goals for treatment.

24. Gives process directives in session and outside of session (e.g., homework) to help the client take steps toward new emotional and/or interpersonal experiences and understandings.

### Time-Limited Aspects of Therapy

25. Discusses the time-limited nature of the therapy in light of the client's CMP and new adaptive narrative. (VTSS 21)

---

*Numbers in parentheses refer to the item number from the original Vanderbilt Therapeutic Strategies Scale (VTSS), reprinted with permission of S. F. Butler. In some cases content from an original item has been combined with that from another item(s) and/or has been altered to include more of an emotional or attachment focus.

therapy in general and in TLDP in particular, it is critical to assess, use, and comment on the strengths of the client to foster change (**Strategy 3**). Often clients are the last to know about their own capacities. No one has ever commented on them, elicited them, admired them; therefore, clients are often blind to their own cognitive, emotional, and relational resources. Highlighting their internal and external resources can often build a strong positive alliance.

In **Strategy 4** the therapist addresses "obstacles" (e.g., coming late) and "opportunities" (e.g., willingness to be vulnerable) that might influence the therapeutic process. In psychoanalytically oriented therapies, "covert or overt opposition to the therapist, the counseling process, or the therapist's agenda" (Bischoff & Tracey, 1995, p. 488) has been called *resistance*. Resistance from the perspective of TLDP, on the other hand, is viewed within the interpersonal sphere—as one of a number of transactions between therapist and client (Levenson, 1995). The assumption is that clients are doing what they believe is necessary to maintain their personal integrity, ingrained perceptions of themselves, and interpersonal connectedness. Resistance in this light reflects the clients' attempts to do the best they can given how they construe the world. For example, a client might miss a session following the session when she has cried in the hour because she is so worried that the therapist will perceive her as too needy.

Thus, when TLDP therapists feel as if they have hit a wall of resistance from the client, they can stand back, appreciate the attachment-based significance of the wall, and invite the client to look at possible "good" reasons to have the wall. Such an approach often avoids power plays with hostile clients and helps to promote empathy and collaboration.

## Accessing and Processing Emotion

No matter what else the therapist may do in the therapy, he or she is trying to relate to clients in the here-and-now of the therapeutic relationship from a deeply empathic place, helping to keep clients in an emotionally receptive "working space" through what has been called *dyadic regulation* (e.g., Tronick, 1989). Such transactions are hypothesized to be beneficial in and of themselves in that they permit emotional processing and the modulation of goal-directed behaviors and adaptive strategies. However, as pointed out by Binder (2004) and others (e.g., Henry et al., 1993b), helping clients stay emotionally regulated (**Strategy 5**) is easier said than done when one is interacting with powerful interpersonal dynamics that dysregulate the therapist's own emotional state. Thus, this strategy is more of a desired optimum therapeutic stance that will usually be manifested through several other specific interventions.

For **Strategy 6,** the therapist actively encourages clients to experience and express affect in the session. Activating the emotional fabric of the person's CMP is critical in changing it. As Greenberg is fond of saying, "You must arrive at a place before you can leave it." From experiential theory, research, and practice, we know that emotional arousal and expression are necessary precursors of change (e.g., Greenberg, 2002; Johnson, 2004). Similarly the therapist helps clients become aware of emotions on the edge of awareness and helps them deepen their emotional experience (**Strategy 7**). However, mere ventilation of emotions is not enough, and the therapist must help clients label their emotional experience and tune into its goal-directed significance (**Strategy 8**). In particular, the TLDP therapist is invested in focusing on the client's accessing, experiencing, and deepening any attachment-related feelings specifically related to the person's CMP (**Strategy 9**).

## Empathic Exploration

Open-ended questions (**Strategy 10**) and inquiring into the personal meanings of the clients' words (**Strategy 11**) as well as asking for concrete details (**Strategy 12**) all help the therapist understand the client's world from the inside out. It is not unusual when I am listening to the client talk in a global fashion about a disturbing (or rewarding) interaction with another person ("She just really ticked me off!") to ask them to slow the action down so that I can understand the details of the situation—both in terms of external transactions and internal, visceral responses.[11] Often clients are quite surprised to see all the steps (e.g., attributions of self and other) that have led them to their reaction that often feels as if it "just happens."

---

[11] It is quite ironic that often my feedback to trainees learning to work briefly is to "slow down" the process.

## Focused Inquiry

Throughout the therapy, the TLDP therapist attempts to maintain a circumscribed line of inquiry and stays on the focus unless there are dramatic indications to the contrary (**Strategy 13**). Such a focusing, however, should not be done in a dogmatic or controlling manner. Binder (2004) defines problem formulation and focusing to be one of the five competencies in conducting good interpersonal–psychodynamic therapy. And as pointed out in Chapter 1, maintaining a focus is the most commonly mentioned feature defining brief dynamic therapy. The TLDP therapist uses the emotional–interpersonal goals derived from the formulation to keep the therapy on track. Such focusing is critical in a brief therapy that demands making the best use of time.

## Relationship Focus

The TLDP therapist encourages clients to talk about their relationships with others (including with the therapist). Focusing on relevant thoughts, feelings, and beliefs associated with such transactions is of paramount importance (**Strategy 14**). Much of the therapeutic work will focus on the clients' relationships *outside of the sessions* (unless a negative process emanating from within the sessions needs to be addressed directly). Similarly, the therapist helps clients explore their perceptions of how the therapist might be acting, feeling, or thinking about them (**Strategy 15**). In this way, the therapeutic relationship is examined as a here-and-now microcosm of what might happen with others.

In a reciprocal fashion, it can often be helpful for therapists to self-disclose their countertransference in response to clients' specific behaviors (**Strategy 16**). Of course the therapist is always self-disclosing inadvertently through gestures, voice quality, facial expression, etc. Self-disclosure is "not an option; it is an inevitability" (Aron, 1991, p. 40). But here I am talking about the therapist's *self-involving disclosures*—statements in the present tense that describe the therapist's reactions to some aspect of the client's CMP (McCarthy & Betz, 1978). In this way the therapist can open up other possibilities in the clients' perceptions of others and help clients appreciate their impact on others. In TLDP therapists need to become comfortable with comprehending their own internal processes and then deciding when, where, and how to share these with clients. TLDP advocates limited self-disclosure specifically designed to give clients more information about the dynamics involved in relating to others. Such disclosures can be narrowly seen as a manifestation of the therapist's *clinical honesty* (Wilkinson & Gabbard, 1993, p. 282).

In particular, the therapist focuses on his or her reactions to the client that are particularly relevant for the client's CMP. It should be noted that the therapist's sharing such reactions is not only helpful for bringing into awareness negative aspects when there are reenactments, but also for recognizing when there are *positive shifts* in the quality of the interaction. For example, after Mrs. Follette (the guarded client described earlier) allowed herself to be more open in session, the therapist shared that he felt closer to her. The reader is referred to Levenson (1995) for a discussion of this type of interactive self-disclosure as distinguished from other types of disclosures.

Related to self-disclosing strategies is *metacommunication* (**Strategy 17**). From an interpersonalist position (Kiesler, 1996), metacommunication involves discussing and processing what occurs in the here-and-now client–therapist relationship that involves both therapist and client. For example, "It seems, Mr. Johnson, as you get quieter and quieter, I become more and more reassuring. I am not sure what is happening here, but can we take a look at what this feels like for both of us?" Muran's (2001) expansion of the definition of metacommunication to include *intrapersonal* aspects (i.e., communication with parts of the self) is also useful. From an attachment point of view, metacommunication can be pivotal in providing corrective emotional experiences, shifts in self-awareness, and richer narratives of the self in relation to self and others.

While much of the therapy will be devoted to examining the clients' issues in their relationships outside the therapy (especially for those with more flexible working models), the therapist's observations about manifestations of the CMP (not necessarily full-blown reenactments) *in the sessions* provides an in vivo understanding of the client's behaviors and stimulus value. By ascertaining how an interpersonal pattern has emerged in the therapeutic relationship, the client has, perhaps for the first time, the opportunity to examine the nature of such behaviors in a relatively safe environment.

I want to make a comment here about the use of *transference interpretations*, since they have been a standard intervention strategy for psychodynamic therapists in both short- and long-term therapies (although intersubjective, two-person approaches like TLDP shy away from using them). When therapists are "analyzing the transference," they are linking emotionally charged interactions with past significant others (usually parents) with what is happening in present transactions between therapist and client, rather than making observations about the ongoing therapeutic process. For example, if I would have *explained* to Mr. Johnson that "you want me to nurture and take care of you in ways you didn't get from your parents," this would be an example of a transference interpretation.

Hill and colleagues (2008) differentiate between immediacy (her term for metacommunication) and transference interpretations in a similar manner:

> Immediacy seeks to promote the *here-and-now awareness* of problematic interpersonal patterns and to create a corrective emotional experience by establishing new interpersonal patterns. By contrast, transference interpretations seek to promote the client's awareness of the existence and insight into the origin of displaced interactional patterns by *providing an explanation* or reason for the behaviors. (Kasper, Hill, & Kivlighan, 2008, p. 282, emphasis added)

I very much like quoting Strupp's admonition that the supply of transference interpretations far exceeds the demand. A few go a long way. In part I have placed a major focus in TLDP on experiential learning and empathic attunement, because of the deleterious effect repeated transference interpretations can have on psychotherapeutic process and outcome. Clients often experience such interventions as blaming and/or belittling (Henry et al., 1993a; Piper, Azim, Joyce, & McCallum, 1991). There is convincing empirical evidence that questions the heretofore prominent role transference interpretations have played in psychodynamic interventions (Henry et al., 1993; Hoglend, Johannsson, Marble, Bogwald, & Amlo, 2007; Piper et al., 1991).

## Exploration of Maladaptive Cyclical Patterns

In **Strategy 18,** the therapist helps clients explore their introjects (how they feel about and treat themselves) and how these relate to their interpersonal patterns (CMPs). Inquiring about how one feels about oneself during certain interpersonal behaviors (especially those that are attachment-related) links one's sense of self with transactions with others. As I say to Ann in the clinical case to follow, "How do you feel about yourself when you cry yourself to sleep, making sure that your boyfriend does not hear you?"

The therapist then helps clients put all of the aforementioned emotional–interpersonal information of self and others into describing a cyclical pattern (**Strategy 19**). For example:

> So when you feel so alone and depressed, and expect no one will be there for you, you make sure that you present yourself as "together," "cool," and not "needy." Is that right? The problem is that others get the message that you don't want their attention, and so they leave you alone. Yes? You see people aren't there for you, and you then tell yourself that no one would want to be with someone so needy, and this makes you feel more depressed, and the whole cycle begins again. Do I have that right?

It is very important at this stage that the therapist be as specific as possible and slowly review each component of the pattern, checking it out with clients at each linking, soliciting their elaboration and emotional confirmation.

Once the pattern has been recognized, the therapist refers to the CMP throughout the therapy and, at each link, helps the client access, experience, and deepen the attachment-related feelings (**Strategy 20**). The therapist focuses on previously warded-off, unacknowledged, disowned, or disavowed attachment-related feelings and/or primary emotions specifically relevant to the CMP. The therapist confronts blocks in experiencing by using experiential techniques such as arousal, heightening, and empathic conjecture (Johnson, 2004). In this way, the client comes to understand the deeper, attachment-based needs that drive the maladaptive cycle and begins to appreciate how this working model has colored his or her worldview.

When appropriate, the therapist then links the need for disowning these primary emotions to the clients' early experiences (**Strategy 21**). The clients come to understand how they perceived these basic core emotions as undesirable by caregivers; therefore, these emotions were suppressed and finally disowned so that early attachments would not be threatened. The therapist can help *depathologize* the client's current behavior and symptoms by explaining how they were a way to survive emotionally as a child, but now they serve no useful purpose and may even be alienating.

Over time, the therapist helps the client incorporate more core feelings (Fosha, 2000) and more adaptive thoughts and behaviors into a new coherent narrative that opens up an expanded sense of self and a wider repertoire of actions, leading to greater intrapersonal and interpersonal health (**Strategy 22**). Going back to our example of Mr. Johnson, by the end of therapy, he was able to talk about how he had to squelch his angry feelings as a child to avoid being beaten by his alcoholic father—a very different narrative than when he entered therapy and shamefully saw himself as weak. In his last session, Mr. Johnson said he now felt entitled to be angry—"honest anger."

## Promoting Change Directly

One of the most important TLDP treatment strategies is providing opportunities for clients to have new experiences in session that are designed to help undermine their CMPs (**Strategy 23**). Therapists should seize opportunities to expand or deepen experiences that disconfirm clients' intrapersonal and interpersonal schemata. The therapist makes clear and repeated efforts to promote such experiential learning (e.g., facilitating new behaviors that the client sees as "risky"). With sufficient quality and/or quantity of these experiences, clients can foster healthier internalized working models of relationships. In this way TLDP promotes change by altering the basic infrastructure of the client's transactional world, which then reverberates to influence the concept of self.

Going back to our case of Mr. Johnson, at one point in the sixth session, he was complaining that he could not think and participate in the therapy because he had not eaten breakfast. When I asked him what he wanted to do, he was confused by my question. Of course he would finish the session!

Upon further inquiry, I learned that he thought I would be angry if he left the session early to get something to eat, and he would want to avoid my anger at all costs. When I simply stated back to him that it seemed he was choosing to remain in the session and be uncomfortable hoping not to displease me, he said he would go get some food if *I* thought it were a good idea. I expressed my curiosity about his leaving the decision up to me by stating in a puzzled tone, "If *I* thought it was a good idea?"

A short while later, Mr. Johnson said he felt better and would finish the session. However, in the next session a similar dynamic (but with different content) arose, and that time, Mr. Johnson announced that he wanted to leave the session early to attend to his personal needs (i.e., take a stool softener so he would not be constipated later that evening when his children came to visit). Rather than interpreting what I thought was going on at an unconscious level, I simply told Mr. Johnson I would look forward to seeing him at our usual time next week. Mr. Johnson's stating his own needs over what he imagined were my wishes (that he should stay in the session no matter what) had been a big risk for him because, as I learned later, he thought I was going to throw him out of therapy if he were not "compliant." Being aware that he was directly verbalizing his own needs (for once in his life), taking a chance that I would disapprove and might even retaliate, and then finding out that his assertiveness did not jeopardize our relationship was a major new intrapersonal *and* interpersonal experience for Mr. Johnson.

However, I do not want to give the impression that in TLDP the therapist tries to create that *one* new experience that totally realigns the client's affective and cognitive world. Rather, new experiences should be encountered throughout the therapy—sometimes as almost imperceptible nuances embedded in the relationship context. In our long-term follow-up study of clients who have received TLDP (Bein et al., 1994), many clients described that one of the biggest benefits they got from therapy was having the opportunity to be more in touch with their emotions as they related in new and healthier ways to their therapists.

Unlike many long-term psychodynamic models, in TLDP the therapist may give directives to help clients foster their growth *outside of the session* (**Strategy 24**). Giving homework, for example, is very compatible with the TLDP approach. However, before making any such assignments, the TLDP therapist must carefully weigh the implications of such directives to make sure they are not a subtle reenactment of the client's dysfunctional pattern. For example, asking Mr. Johnson to take assertiveness training classes may sound like a good idea on the surface. But if it is something he does because he feels he must do whatever I say in order to stay in my good graces, the homework assignment just serves to feed his attachment fears and compliant security operations—ultimately making sure he has yet another dysfunctional interpersonal interaction.

## Time-Limited Aspects

**Strategy 25** involves the therapist's introducing and discussing the time-limited or brief nature of the therapy. The brief therapist does not do this just at the end of the treatment. At the beginning of the work and periodically throughout, the TLDP therapist comments on the limits on the time and/or scope of the work. TLDP, however, is not one of those models (like that of Mann, 1973, introduced in Chapter 2) that emphasizes the finiteness of time in order to precipitate change. Rather, it is thought of as the backdrop against which dysfunctional patterns take center stage. As termination approaches, one can expect to see the client's anxiety about loss handled in ways characteristic for that particular person given his or her CMP. Painful emotions associated with previous losses can be evoked. However, the TLDP therapist does not stray from the overarching goals of the treatment.

Given the TLDP systems framework, when one person (the client) changes, other people's responses are affected, usually reinforcing the client's positive changes. As previously mentioned, I think of the therapeutic work continuing after the sessions have ended. For example, with Mr. Johnson, where there used to be a vicious dysfunctional cycle, now there was more of a victorious cycle filled with energy and joy. As a consequence of his feeling more powerful in the world, he began socializing more. He experienced himself as more alive and involved in life; his self-pity and depressive thinking were dramatically decreased. Now that he was a happier person, his adult children enjoyed being around him more, which only served to quiet his fears of abandonment and reinforce his sense of security. A year after he ended treatment, during a follow-up interview (done by another therapist), I learned that Mr. Johnson had moved into a house owned by two other people. After living there a short time, he had been instrumental in setting up a rule that if any tension occurred among the housemates, they would sit down at the dining room table and talk about it after dinner. For a man who had been so conflict-avoidant, this was a clearly a sign of further growth. The therapy continued in Mr. Johnson's life, although the sessions had ended a year ago.

How does the therapist make a good decision about knowing when a client is "ready" to end?[12] As one of the originators of single-session therapy, Michael Hoyt (Hoyt, Rosenbaum, & Talmon, 1992), has said to me, "Clients are not 'done'; they are not baked like a cake!" In brief therapy, we are clearly not looking for therapeutic perfectionism. All of the loose ends are not tied together. However, since brief therapy often ends while the client usually is in the midst of changing, I have six sets of questions to help guide beginning brief therapists in making termination decisions as the therapy is proceeding:[13]

- Has the client evidenced interactional changes with significant others in his or her life? Are these transactions more rewarding?
- Does the client evidence more emotional fluidity within himself or herself? Does the client report a fuller experience of self?
- Has the client had a new experience (or a series of new experiences) of himself or herself and the therapist within the therapy?

---

[12] I have found that having an explicit ending date (rather than a fixed number of sessions or a brief therapy defined by a limited focus) works best for training. With a fixed date, therapists-in-training are forced to confront their "resistances" to working briefly (Hoyt, 1985)—for example, fears of being seen as withholding, the need to be needed, and overconcern for "successful" termination. Also when I do group supervision with a specific termination date, all the trainees are roughly on the same page—beginning and ending together. Without such a structure, I have found that beginning brief therapists often find "good reasons" for extending the length of the therapy.

[13] Unfortunately, in today's managed care environment, the decision of when to end therapy is often not made collaboratively between therapist and client. Instead it may be a decision made by an administrative person or limited by one's insurance coverage to a specified number of sessions for specific diagnoses. See Levenson and Burg (2000) for a discussion of the effect of these economic influences on professional training and patient care.

- Has there been a change in the level on which the therapist and client are relating (usually from parent–child to adult–adult)?
- Has the therapist's countertransferential reaction to the client shifted (usually from negative to positive)?
- Does the client manifest some understanding about his or her dynamics and the role he or she needed to play to maintain them?

If the answer to most of these questions is no, then I do not consider that the client has had an adequate course of TLDP. The therapist should consider why this has been the case and weigh the possible benefits of using another therapeutic model, another course of TLDP, a different therapist, nonpsychological interventions, and so forth.

## Case Example

I wish to discuss the case of Ann, the young woman who was kind enough to allow me to work with her in therapy for six sessions that were videotaped for the American Psychological Association's series Psychotherapy in Six Sessions.[14] Ann is a 25-year-old, attractive, thin, single, white woman with short curly hair. She enters the first session all bubbly and smiling.

### Session One

There is much to accomplish in a first session of a brief dynamic therapy. The therapist sets the time frame (for each individual session length and for the length of the therapy in total); assesses the client's appropriateness for a brief dynamic approach; attempts to establish safety and collaboration with the client fostering a therapeutic alliance; listens for relational themes in the content and process of what the client is presenting so that a rudimentary, initial focus may be discerned; becomes aware of how he

---

[14] All six sessions of my therapy with this client are available on DVD through the American Psychological Association (APA) Publications Department, Phone: (202) 336-5510; E-mail: order@apa.org; Internet: www.apa.org/books. These six sessions were not set up to be a complete brief dynamic therapy; the six-session format was specified by APA as part of its clinical demonstration series. Nonetheless, I think the work effectively illustrates many of the concepts and interventions of a modern brief dynamic therapy. For this book, several identifying aspects of the case have been altered.

or she is feeling and interacting with the client; and begins delineating the goals for the work. In addition, the client's responses to initial interventions in the first session give an indication of the pacing of the therapy. Hence, *the first session is critical*—brief therapists must formulate and intervene knowing the time is limited; they are motivated to make every session count. The first session captures the essence of a brief therapy; one must proceed on relatively little information and be willing to "lead the client one step behind."[15]

After introducing myself to Ann, I tell her that we will be able to "meet for 45 minutes today and then if I can be of help, we can meet another five times," over the next 3 months, to which she replies enthusiastically, "Oh, great!" I note that she appears cheerfully accommodating to what is a strange setting for such an intimate discussion, since we are being videotaped on a sound stage with bright lights and three cameras pointed at us. She tells me her reason for wanting therapy at this time is that she has been thinking about being in therapy "for years," and "was excited to see how this all works." While she briefly alludes to being "stressed" (i.e., working full time, going to school, and in a long-distance relationship), I am wondering where her pain is—what would motivate her to do an intensive piece of therapeutic work at this time. I sense her "excitement" has an anxious undertone. Of course, there is much in the present fish-bowl setting to cause us both to be anxious. Nonetheless, there is something in her eagerness to please that feels more part of her characteristic style. Given that only 2 minutes have passed, this may seem like a lot of conjecturing for a therapist to do; yet this is this part of how one starts conceptualizing in a brief dynamic model.

Since I am not sure what Ann is hoping to get out of any work we might do together, I simply ask her, "Is there something in particular . . . that concerns you?" Again, this straightforward sentence exemplifies the transparency and directness that often is a part of brief therapy. When she replies, "just the stress level" and her "anxiety," I ask for specifics. For example, how does she experience the anxiety in her body? Having the client focus on

---

[15] I particularly like this phrase of Milton Erickson's because it so nicely phrases the paradox of a brief therapy; the therapist must be willing to give *direction* to the client, but also must *follow* the client's leads.

her somatic sense of self will enable the therapist to assess the client's level of emotional awareness. In addition, it lays the groundwork for facilitating the client's understanding of how emotions are significant for change.

Ann is able to tell me that when she is anxious, she feels her heart and thoughts "racing." This is a good prognostic sign in that she has some awareness of what she is experiencing physically and mentally.[16] Ann also comments that she does not get a good night's sleep and that her boyfriend's alarm clock is "not dependable." This is a curious statement. Why wouldn't an alarm clock be dependable, and if it were truly not reliable, why wouldn't one buy one that is? The thought crosses my mind that perhaps it is her boyfriend that is not dependable. I am not attached to this thought, but I am intrigued by associations, metaphors, and images that the client or I might have—all aspects that do not depend on explicit, linguistically mediated ideas.

I am keenly aware of my own thoughts and feelings as I interact with Ann. My *interactive countertransference* as I step into a relationship with the client informs me of what others might experience relating to her and also gives me a window into what she might be experiencing. At the outset I am relieved that she seems to be "nice" and "cooperative"[17] but also suspect that there is more here than meets the eye.

I also take note of the mismatch between the content of what Ann is saying and her presentational style. She is smiling broadly and nodding enthusiastically. If one were watching the video of this session without the volume, there would be little indication of the negative things she is relating. The disparity between the way she is talking (cheerfully) and what she is talking about (being tired, stressed, and overwhelmed) is another clue as to where we might need to go therapeutically. I think to myself, *where* and *when* did she learn to keep private how much she is hurting inside? Attachment theory suggests to me possible reasons *why* she may have

---

[16] With clients who are not aware of what is going on in their bodies, the therapist needs to start there. Gendlin's focusing work or Greenberg's experiential processing approach is helpful in this regard. Also see Levenson (1995) for a discussion of alexithymia and brief therapy.

[17] Book's (1998) conceptualization of a unique form of countertransference is applicable here. He speaks of "in press countertransference" as a therapist's wish for a case to be a successful demonstration of a particular psychotherapy method so that it can be used as a case illustration in a book.

needed to hide her pain (from others and possibly from herself)—perhaps it was not accepted by her caregivers or significant others in her life and, therefore, needed to be suppressed and/or disowned.

I am conscious of being intrigued and feel some hope that Ann and I could do a meaningful piece of work—even in six sessions. Specifically, I am encouraged because she is answering my queries, demonstrating trust in me and in the process, and sharing in a revealing manner what is going on at a visceral level. I feel engaged, pulled in emotionally by her style, and start to discern a pattern in the content of what she is saying and the process of how she is saying it.

I proceed to check out if this "stress" she is experiencing is acute or more long lasting. Her reply ("That's been my life every since I can remember") resonates with my sense. I then turn to gauging her resourcefulness and ask her how she has tried to deal with her anxiety in the past. This might not only give me an idea as to her strengths, but also an indication of what might not be helpful. Ann tells me about an area of pride—that she has changed her eating patterns to become healthier ("Now I crave better foods"). I am delighted to hear this, not only because it connotes that she is motivated for self-care and changing long-existing behaviors, but also that it provides us with a metaphor for how she might want to "nourish" other parts of herself. I reframe this back to her as, "It sounds like feeling strong in your own skin is very important to you now," creating a bridge from the physiological realm to the psychological. A little while later, Ann confirms, "It is important for me to be an overall strong person and independent person in all aspects." I am aware that I do not experience her as an independent person—rather, I have a sense based on her presentation thus far that she would go a long way to please me (and others). I entertain the idea that she is conveying a wish—a self as she would like to be. I have gone into some detail describing what are only minutes of a first session to illustrate that from a TLDP therapist's point of view, formulation is already under way.

I begin to do an *anchored history*, following what Ann is saying, asking for more detail, expanding it forward and backward in time. In this way, I get a trajectory, context, and thickening of her life's story. For example, when she talks about her family, I ask her if there is anything about her childhood she would have liked to have been different, and I hear that she wished she had had friends. As I explore this missing aspect of her youth, I find out that she was terribly hurt by a childhood chum (a past significant other) who pushed her away. In session, I conjecture (in a way designed to heighten any underlying emotion) that perhaps she made a vow to herself that she was not going to let herself get hurt like that ever again.[18] Ann confirms this ("Because I wasn't getting my needs met; she wasn't reciprocating. I have a hard time with that") and elaborates that "I feel like I am always the one giving . . . and sometimes I don't feel like I am getting anything back."

I then take what seems to be coalescing into a recognizable relational theme and ask if it manifests with her boyfriend (a present significant other), to which she empathically replies, "Absolutely!" With this her voice trembles, and I simply ask her in a soft, slow-paced voice pointing at my own chest, "What is going on inside with you right now?" She is no longer the bubbly, effervescent ingénue. She says she is frustrated and apologizes—both the feeling and the behavior are noteworthy. Women in our society often experience frustration when they are angry because it is socially frowned on for women to be aggressive; therefore, I wonder if her frustration comes from censored, suppressed, or disowned angry feelings. In addition, she is apologizing to me as though expressing her frustration would be unacceptable.

Following this, I link her behavior (acts of self) to her experience of her boyfriend (acts of others) in the first person. "Why isn't he going out of his way for me? I go out of my way for him! Why isn't he giving when it is not convenient?" Ann cries wholeheartedly when I say this and sobs, "I give and I give and I want something back!" When Ann exclaims this through her tears, I feel the power, truth, and integrity (congruence between what she is saying and how she is saying it) of what she is sharing with me. I am getting the sense that this claiming of what she wants is the beginning of some new experiential learning for her, already evident in the first few minutes of the first session.

---

[18] My phrasing (i.e., "I have made a vow of never, never again will I be put in this position") has been influenced by an intervention used by Johnson (2004).

A little while later, I lead Ann in an exploration of how she acts with her boyfriend and learn (not surprisingly) that she does not let him know how much she is hurt by his self-centered behavior. She volunteers that she is "scared" to let him know—"afraid he will leave. I will say my needs and he will leave" (*expectations of others' behaviors*). Here we have a possible root of her attachment fear—that if she expresses fully who she is, she will be rejected. This leads me to ask about the fourth component of the CMP (*acts of the self toward the self*)—"It sounds like somehow you don't believe that you would be enough; that he really just loves the you that is giving, giving, giving." And she confirms, "Yes, I have to keep giving to make sure I am enough for him. I absolutely feel that way."

We are not quite 30 minutes into the session, and I am helping her piece together the links between her dysfunctional behaviors, self-defeating expectations, the way she is responded to, and her negative self-appraisals (i.e., the four components of the CMP). *Interpersonal theory* helps me trace the transactional patterns; *attachment theory* provides me an understanding of her longing for relational felt security and safety; and emotionally focused, *experiential theory* keeps me attuned to the expression and understanding of her primary emotions that will be the fulcrum of substantial and long-lasting change. While my skills of observation and recognition have been honed over 30 years of doing clinical work, neophyte brief therapists can use the same five categories of the CMP and the same three theoretical foci that I am using. These provide a structure by which to make sense of the flood of information and to direct the therapist's attention.

The redundancy of Ann's interpersonal behaviors that occur across people, place, and time form the rudimentary CMP that I convey to Ann by the end of the first session. "You're up against a pattern that you have established over your life to be okay. But now it's not okay—that way of operating in the world—that giving, giving is not okay right now. You want something more. Uh oh, if I dare ask for something more, what's going to happen? So an important time for you."

In this summation, I am doing a number of important things consistent with the TLDP model. I am naming that this is a pattern—helping her see things within a different narrative—a narrative that has form, internal logic, and hope. In addition, by focusing on a patterned cycle, I am externalizing the problem—the problem is this pattern, not Ann herself. Furthermore, in keeping with the nonpathologizing stance of TLDP, I am validating that Ann has good reasons to have co-created this pattern in her life, because it helped her feel "okay." I am also supporting the idea that this pattern of giving and giving is not working for her now, and that she wants something more. This statement takes us from a focus on understanding what keeps her stuck (the pattern that is causing her pain) to the idea that she wants something to shift. Finally, I am also underscoring that such change is scary and not to be taken lightly, while acknowledging that it is important.

Before leaving this discussion of the first session, I want to make two last points. First, while I feel rather confident about discerning an emerging pattern, I am holding all of it lightly, ready to change any and all of this rudimentary formulation depending upon what I hear, see, or sense next. Second, the goals for this therapy are process- and not content-based. For a successful treatment, it is not necessary for Ann to break up with her boyfriend. Rather what is important is that she is encouraged to have *new experiences* and *new understandings* designed to help free her from rigidly adhering to certain emotional and behavioral dysfunctional patterns.

Specifically, given her pattern of pleasing others at the cost of suppressing her own emotional truth, my tentative plan is to focus interventions on helping Ann experience herself as more worthwhile (*introject*) and more entitled to speak her mind, heart, and gut in an assertive manner (*acts of the self*). In addition, I would like for her to experience me as interested in her for herself and not because I need her to take care of me (*acts of others*). According to the TLDP model, these experiential goals address her intrapersonal and interpersonal life. By the end of the therapy, I would also want her to have an understanding of how suppressing her own feelings gives her a diminished sense of self (*introject*), and behaving in unauthentic ways (*acts of self*) only serves to invite the very response she so fears (*acts of others*) while depriving her of her own emotional compass.

A brief therapist is always aware of the time-limited aspects of the therapy and conveys this to clients at various junctures. At the end of the first session, I tell Ann that we have five more sessions if she would like to continue working with me. Ann enthusiastically and wholeheartedly says, "I'd love to!" I am very aware here and throughout the session that it would be in keeping with Ann's style for her to attempt to please me. I remind myself that as the therapy goes forward I will need to stay alert to times when I am hooked into reenacting a dysfunctional dynamic with her—pulled to behave in certain ways by her pleasant, pleasing stance.

I close the session by telling Ann that "I think you've been very forthcoming and really told your story in a way that I am already getting a feel for what you are wrestling with. It sounds like it was a courageous act to come in." In this way, I am supporting Ann's strengths in confronting these emotional demons that have plagued her for so long. In doing TLDP, it is critical to convey to clients and to frame for them that doing a focused, intensive piece of work takes emotional energy and fortitude and that the therapist realizes and respects this.

I think quite a bit has been accomplished in this first session. Ann appears to be a good candidate for TLDP, meeting all five selection criteria (see Chapter 2). We seem to have the beginnings of a good alliance. I am already getting a sense of Ann's dysfunctional interpersonal pattern and have some ideas about the goals for the therapy. I also have a hypothesis about how her dysfunctional pattern might manifest itself in the session (*transference–countertransference reenactments*) with her trying to be the "good patient."

### Session Two

In the second session I let Ann set the agenda, but I am mindful of my working formulation and am already listening to her through this filter. The topics evolve from stress in school to her describing herself as the "clingy girlfriend." At this point I share how from a cultural perspective girls in our society are given the message that their needs are not that important. She speaks about how she tries to model for her boyfriend that giving is good, but I gently confront her when I say, "Well, modeling is one way of showing someone, but then there is something that is keeping you from really letting him know what is really going on with you."

A bit later, I open up the area of attachment fears by saying, "Somewhere you learned over the years, and I know society plays a role, but somewhere you learned you need to keep giving and giving and keep your fingers crossed that the other person is going to come around." With this empathic conjecture,[19] Ann begins to tell the story of how her mother drank heavily while she was growing up.

Ann's face contorts and she sobs as she tells me, "I have been wanting her to quit for years. Because there would be times she would come home and pass out, and I would sit on the floor next to her—to make sure she is breathing. I was afraid she would throw up and die." I am very moved as she describes this, and I get an image of a small child crouched on the floor, feeling incredibly terrified and totally responsible for keeping her mother alive. I reply softly, "It doesn't get any bigger than that for a child—wondering if a parent is going to die on them."

Because of her reluctance to tell her boyfriend of her pain, I ask if she ever told her mother about what she was going through emotionally as a child. Not surprisingly, Ann responds, "No." As the session comes to an end, I frame for her a different story than she has been telling herself all these years. I let her know that she is "wrestling with trying to do it differently—to honor yourself and your feelings. But it is difficult. The fears, the fears I can better understand now—the fears from when you were a little girl—fears about will there be anyone here to take care of me. . . . I can see where you would put your needs way down because those were very big stakes. Who wants their mother to die on them? . . . I can see where you learned those lessons very young."

By the time the session ends, Ann has the idea that she is dealing with an "old, old pattern," but patterns that get rewoven in her *present* life. Now the enemy is not herself and her inadequacies, but rather that she learned a way of being that made sense at the time, but now does not serve her well. Of course during all of this exploration, I am mindful of being very present with her and empathic with her pain, providing the beginnings of a corrective emotional experience.

---

[19] This is another technique used in experiential–process therapy.

Session Three

In the third session, Ann comes in with her leg in a brace; she had had a knee replacement 2 days ago. When I acknowledge that such surgery can be pretty painful (coincidentally, I had had the same surgery on the same knee the previous year), she says, "It's better that it hurts now and we'll fix it, or it will hurt forever." I wonder to myself if this statement also applies to her goals for therapy, so I say, "Sometimes it is hard to go through the acute pain and know in your mind it's going to get better," again speaking to her on two levels—the physical (her surgery) and the psychological (her therapy).

I ask her if there is anything on her mind she was hoping to work on in this session. On one level this is a focusing intervention, and on another I am trying to give her another new experience (i.e., this is *her* time to use as she sees fit). She starts talking about how she fears that now that she cannot exercise (due to her recuperation), she might regain some weight she had worked so hard to lose.

At this point in our work together, my concern that Ann might have an eating disorder is growing. I use her reference to exercise to explore this possibility. While the main focus for the TLDP therapist is the client's interpersonal patterns, he or she cannot overlook other conditions that might hinder the functioning of the client. Once I am satisfied that she does not seem have an eating problem, I pivot the content of the session in a different direction, exploring how she is different from others in her family.

Later when watching the videotape of this session, I could see if she were more assertive, she might have confronted me at this point to let me know that I was not addressing her fear of gaining weight. Was Ann subverting her own needs in order to meet mine? If I would have been aware of this possible reenactment in the session, I might have processed (metacommunicated about) it with her in real time by saying something like, "I notice that I have taken our discussion away from your stated concerns; I wonder how that happened" (interpersonal focus). Or "I notice that I have taken our discussion away from your stated concerns; I'm wondering how you're feeling about that" (intrapersonal focus)." Or "I realized I was worried about your health" (self-disclosure).

By the middle of the third session, I have heard segments of Ann's pattern several times, which encourages me to link these emotions and personal meanings into a CMP and propose it to her as relevant to her most important *current* relationship. "Everything is planned to keep from getting hurt. To be how he would like you to be, so then he will be there. He won't leave you. Because if you were who you are, the fear is that he would leave. You really believe that, yes?" Here I state her abandonment fear, simply and boldly, and I can tell from her emotional response—her eyes welling up and breaking into sobs—that she grasps the essence of what I am saying. Through her tears she describes a vivid and poignant image—"Like you reach out and no one is there."

As we near the midway point in our work together (end of third session), I propose that she "experiment" coming forward with someone in her life who is "safe enough." We collaborate on a homework assignment of her letting a new girlfriend know a bit more about her—for her to actually take up space instead of just being the accommodating listener. One usually does not think of homework assignments in psychodynamically oriented therapy, but when one is working briefly and needing to make every session count, having the client take interpersonal risks *outside of the session* is an excellent way of speeding the process in a real and relevant way.

For the remaining three sessions we continue working on the same CMP that gets further elaborated and refined. My goals remain an overriding focus, and I find no reason in what she says to change them.

### Sessions Four and Five

In the fourth session, Ann relates how she felt the homework was a "success." She was able to talk to her girlfriend "mostly about me," and she is "really excited" that it went well. I reflect back, "So you took a risk and what you feared would happen didn't happen."

In the fifth session, I remind her that it is our "next to last session." I introduce an examination of ways in which she felt her customary patterns may have emerged in our relationship. Ann talks about initially feeling pulled to "do a good job" in the sessions "to make your job a little easier." However, now just a few sessions later, we both agree that "it's definitely changed." Ann exclaims that "it feels great, because I'm not overanalyzing anything, really! When I go home, I analyze it, but not in the moment." In this penultimate session, Ann talks about how she has started journaling (on her own) about the "pros and cons" of her with and without her "walls"—her being the "fake person" versus her being "intimately close" by "just being myself, not having to pretend to be someone else." Such self-reflection and learning between sessions are essential facets of a brief dynamic treatment.

### Session Six

In our last session, Ann talks about how in the preceding week she took "a little baby step" toward asserting her needs with her boyfriend. "I wanted him to understand that [his behavior] hurt me." Her feared outcome of being abandoned did not occur. In fact, "he held me [and] tried to make me feel better. Which is nice, because I don't usually say anything. . . . He didn't run away. I noticed that." Although such a specific action was never a concrete goal of this TLDP, it is a dramatic manifestation of how far she has come in opening up options for herself to have more positive interpersonal outcomes. "I always wanted to have a connection with people, but I was afraid to do that . . . and with [my boyfriend] to be able to do that in six sessions was just unheard of. I never would have done that . . . but instead I have done a 180 and I like it!"

In final sessions, I always like to address how the person will continue with the work begun in therapy. Anticipating difficulties is one such way. In the last session, I say to Ann, "There will be another situation where something comes up and you start having a feeling—a strong feeling—feeling hurt or anger or resentment. Can we talk about something you can do right then, rather than suppress that emotion?"

Of course, in this last session we need to say our good-byes. It has been a meaningful, interactive experience between us—not just as client and therapist, but also as two individuals who held each other in each other's mind and who risked being emotionally present. With a couple of minutes left in the session, Ann says our time together "has gone by really fast. If anyone, even like future therapists, I definitely recommend getting your own therapy. . . . I would love to continue on the outside with another therapist."

Although this was a truncated brief therapy done for demonstration training purposes, in many respects Ann meets the TLDP criteria for termination (discussed in the previous section). She has evidenced more rewarding transactions with others, has had a fuller emotional experience of herself, has had a new interpersonal experience with the therapist, was relating in a more resilient fashion, and has an understanding about the reasons her role relationships with others took a particular form. In addition, my countertransference reaction to her has shifted. I truly felt what I told her at the close of our last session: "It has been a very rich experience for me, and I think you are one courageous lady."

# Evaluation

## EMPIRICAL RESEARCH ON BRIEF DYNAMIC PSYCHOTHERAPY

It should be stated at the outset that almost all psychotherapy research in the United States is based on *brief* therapies that last fewer than 20 sessions (Lambert, Bergin, & Garfield, 2004). In part this is due to the expense involved in conducting long-term studies, but in other ways it reflects that we now know "that a good deal of change can be stimulated in a much shorter time than previously thought" (p. 814). Thus, when we talk about research studies on brief therapy, to a large extent we are referring to what we know about therapy in general.[1]

### Does Brief Therapy Work?

Findings from a number of studies from the 1950s to the present have repeatedly shown that the more therapy the better (Hansen, Lambert, & Forman, 2002; Knekt et al., 2008; Seligman, 1995). We offer something

---

[1] It is certainly beyond the scope of this chapter to review the vast empirical literature on brief dynamic therapy. The reader is referred to overviews by Fonagy, Roth, and Higgitt (2005); Gibbons, Crits-Christoph, & Hearon, 2008; and Lambert, Garfield, and Bergin (2004).

good, and the more of it a client receives, the better the outcome, framing what has been called the *dose-effect relationship* (Howard, Kopta, Krause, & Orlinsky, 1986). However, when one looks at the rate of change over time, what becomes apparent is that significant and meaningful change can occur within a relatively short period of time—that improvement curves are steeper for the first 20 sessions or so and then start to (but not quite) level out. Improvement as measured a variety of ways (e.g., self-report scales, days lost from work, observations of others) is most rapid in early sessions.

Looking at these improvement rates over time (Hansen & Lambert, 2003; Howard et al., 1986; Kadera, Lambert, & Andrews, 1996), it has been estimated that 50% of clients in open-ended therapies showed clinical improvement by sessions 8–16, and 75% by the 26th session (which is within the time frame of most brief therapies). Hansen and colleagues (2002) found that approximately 60–70% of clients improve within 13 sessions.[2]

With regard to the types of clients and problems that can be helped in a brief amount of time (according to what has been called the *phase model*), data indicate subjective well-being shifts first, followed by symptoms, and then characterological and interpersonal changes (Howard, Leuger, Maling, & Martinovich, 1993). Specifically, studies have found that those with acute and chronic symptoms can experience clinically meaningful change in 13–18 sessions, while achieving such results for those with more characterological symptoms may require as much as 30 sessions or more (e.g., Hoglend, 2003; Kopta, Howard, Lowery, & Beutler, 1994). Similarly, while clients with mild to moderate depression may be helped in less than 16 sessions, those who are severely depressed often need more (Shapiro et al., 1995).

---

[2] As previously pointed out in Chapter 1, brief dynamic therapy is not ultra-brief therapy. Research on clients receiving psychological treatment via managed health care organizations where the number of sessions is five or less indicates that fewer than 25% have meaningful improvement (Hansen, Lambert, & Forman, 2002). "These values are far below the number of sessions assumed necessary in clinical trials to produce improvement, let alone recovery" (p. 338). However, Sanderson (2002) observes that perhaps the outcomes were poor in these very brief treatments because the treatments themselves were ineffective. Barkham, Shapiro, Hardy, and Reese (1999) at the Sheffield/Leeds psychotherapy of depression research group found that a substantial proportion of clients with mild depression were helped in three sessions. Clearly future work on the effectiveness of these ultra-brief therapies is warranted, although at present their effectiveness remains to be demonstrated.

A well-controlled study found that by the ninth session of a brief dynamic psychotherapy, clients' sense of well-being changed most fully, followed by decreases in distress, and each of these preceded and separately predicted gains in social and interpersonal functioning (Hilsenroth et al., 2001). Abbass, Sheldon, Gyra, and Kalpin (2008) found that clients diagnosed with personality disorders markedly changed following intensive short-term dynamic psychotherapy (ISTDP), but it should be noted that the average length of treatment was almost 30 sessions. Messer and Kaplan (2004), reviewing the relevant literature on personality-disordered clients, concluded that improvements do occur with brief dynamic therapy, but that "moderate to longer term therapy may be needed for the more severe cases" (p. 113). Encouragingly, therapists specifically trained in brief dynamic approaches and techniques tend to be more helpful to clients (Anderson & Lambert, 1995; Hilsenroth, Defife, Blagys, & Ackerman, 2006).

Meta-analytic studies, which statistically combine findings from a number of studies, indicate that brief dynamic psychotherapy is superior to waiting list control groups and has equivalent outcomes to other psychotherapeutic treatments (e.g., cognitive-behavior therapy, solution-focused therapy) and medication and that its effects are stable (Anderson & Lambert, 1995; Crits-Christoph, 1992; DeMaat et al., 2008; Leichsenring, Rabung, & Leibing, 2004). In a randomized trial on the effectiveness of long- and short-term psychodynamic psychotherapy, Knekt and colleagues (2008) found that the brief treatment group was able to maintain its positive gains during the 3-year follow-up. In keeping with the dose–effect model, the longer-term therapy was more effective, but it took 3 years for this difference to manifest. It is important to note that 20% of the participants in the study withdrew when they learned they were being assigned to the long-term group.

Furthermore, in another study Piper and colleagues (1984) considered the cost–benefit analysis of change and concluded that brief dynamic therapy was better than longer-term treatment when one considered the financial aspects (not to mention the cost in time and effort). Certainly there is more need for randomized controlled designs and naturalistic and process studies on brief dynamic psychotherapies, but considering the consistency of the findings, there is much to encourage the brief dynamic therapy practitioner.

Unfortunately, there has been very little work examining cultural factors and brief therapy outcome and process. It has been found repeatedly that *most people, regardless of their cultural backgrounds, prefer briefer therapies* (Sue, Zane, & Young, 1994). However, until there are research data to inform us, "mental health professionals should exercise caution in using brief models with diverse populations and should adapt them to the unique cultural and social situation of the client" (Welfel, 2004, p. 347). Intriguingly, Levenson and Davidovitz (2000) found that female therapists devoted a significantly greater percentage of their clinical time to long-term psychodynamically oriented therapies than did their male counterparts who were more likely to prefer shorter-term treatments. But it is unknown how this difference might influence outcome.

## Research on Time-Limited Dynamic Psychotherapy

### Process/Outcome Studies

With regard to therapeutic outcome, Travis, Binder, Bliwise, & Horne-Moyer (2001) found that following TLDP, clients significantly shifted in their attachment styles (from insecure to secure) and increased the number of their secure attachment themes. The VA Short-Term Psychotherapy Project (the VAST Project) examined TLDP process and outcome with clients who often had Axis I (psychiatric symptoms), II (personality disorders), *and* III (medical problems) diagnoses (Levenson & Bein, 1993). As part of that project, Overstreet (1993) found that approximately 60% of clients had positive interpersonal or symptomatic outcomes following TLDP (average of 14 sessions). At termination, over 70% of clients felt their problems had lessened.

A VAST Project long-term follow-up study of this population (Bein, Levenson, & Overstreet, 1994; Levenson & Bein, 1993) found that client gains from treatment were maintained and slightly bolstered. In addition, at the time of follow-up, 80% of the clients thought their therapies had helped them deal more effectively with their problems. In a naturalistic effectiveness study of 75 clients treated with TLDP, neurotic and psychosomatic clients evidenced significant improvement at termination, as well as 6-month and 12-month follow-ups (Junkert-Tress, Schnierda, Hartkamp, Schmitz, & Tress, 2001). Those diagnosed with personality disorders also improved, but to a lesser degree.

With regard to therapeutic process, Henry, Schacht, and Strupp (1990) found that for poor outcome cases, therapists communicated in a more hostile fashion, and the degree to which therapists used such hostile and controlling statements was related to the number of clients' self-blaming statements. In addition, those therapists who had a more negative self-image were more likely to treat their clients in a withdrawing (i.e., disaffiliative) manner. And all of this occurred by the third session of therapy! Quintana and Meara (1990) also found that clients came to treat themselves similar to the way their therapists treated them in short-term therapy. A later investigation (Hilliard, Henry, & Strupp, 2000) further demonstrated that how clients and therapists thought about themselves (introjects) had a direct effect on the therapy process, which then affected outcome. Bedics, Henry, and Atkins (2005) found that early in treatment, therapist warmth predicted how clients treated their significant others (more affiliative and less hostile) when the relationship was rated at its best. Clearly these process studies underscore how *the interpersonal affects the intrapersonal and vice versa.*

Johnson, Popp, Schacht, Mellon, and Strupp (1989), using a modification of the CMP, found that reliable relationship themes could be identified. Hartmann and Levenson's (1995) study demonstrated that TLDP case formulation is relevant in a real clinical situation. CMP case formulations written by treating therapists (after the first one or two sessions with their clients) conveyed reliable and valid data to other clinicians. Perhaps most meaningful is their finding that better outcomes were achieved the more the therapists stayed focused on topics relevant to their clients' CMPs.

### Training Effects

Strupp and his research group undertook a direct investigation into the effects of training on therapist performance. Theirs is one of the only studies in this important area. They found that following manualized training in TLDP, therapists' interventions became congruent with TLDP strategies (Henry et al., 1993b), and that these changes held even with the more difficult clients (Henry et al., 1993a). However, a later analysis suggested that many of these therapists did not reach an acceptable level of TLDP mastery (Bein et al., 2000).

Additional findings suggest that training in TLDP needs to include *close, directive, and specific feedback* to professionals learning the model and to focus on the *therapists' own thought processes* during the training (Henry et al., 1993a). Similarly, Hilsenroth (2007) also advocates for more "focused, intensive, and task-specific instructional methods" when teaching short-term dynamic psychotherapy (p. 41).

The training approach I use (Levenson, 1995, 2003) incorporates these guidelines. In my group supervision and didactic seminar, trainees receive specific instruction in TLDP theory, case formulation, and intervention strategies, illustrated by clinical vignettes on video. They are assigned to work with one client for 20 weeks. Trainees are explicitly invited to examine their own affective, behavioral, and cognitive processes as they present and/or listen to cases in class. They write down their case formulations and goals (according to the CMP template reproduced in Chapter 4) and share them with the class. Every week, they present a video segment from their most recent session and ask the class for feedback concerning a particular issue of their choosing (e.g., why a certain intervention did not seem to work, talking about their countertransferential feelings at a particular juncture, or just feeling stuck about what to say). The class and I discuss the trainee's specific questions, while I encourage them to stay aware of the larger issues of maintaining an alliance, keeping the focus, and aligning their interventions with the goals of treatment. Thus, by the end of the 6-month course, each trainee not only has an idea of how brief dynamic therapy works with his or her client, but also how it manifests in the very different therapist–client dyads of their classmates' cases.

Teaching experienced (predominately long-term) therapists to do TLDP revealed that those with more hours of previous supervision were less likely "to change their accustomed style of intervention" (Henry et al., 1993a, p. 446). Regarding the training of beginning therapists, Kivligan and his colleagues (1989) found that the clients of even novice TLDP therapists reported more therapeutic work and more painful feelings than those seen by control counselors, and live supervision was more likely to foster TLDP skills when compared to videotaped supervision (1991). Multon, Kivlighan, and Gold (1996) demonstrated that prepracticum counselor trainees were able to increase their adherence to TLDP strategies with training; furthermore, a related study (Kivlighan, Schuetz, & Kardash, 1998) found that the more trainees focused on learning as an end in itself, they better they did. In another training study, Levenson and Bolter (1988) found that trainees' values and attitudes toward brief therapy became more positive after a 6-month seminar and group supervision in TLDP. Other research has supported these findings with professionals attending brief therapy workshops (Neff, Lambert, Lunnen, Budman, & Levenson, 1997).

In a naturalistic study by Fauth, Smith, and Mathisen (2005), doctoral trainees participated in a 20-week training in TLDP. Findings indicate that while trainees' effectiveness peaked in the training phase, it deteriorated post-training. Based on feedback from the trainees, the investigators concluded that they had failed to take into account the lack of support in the organizational/treatment culture where the students' individual supervisors were not TLDP proponents. In a more recent article on "big ideas" for psychotherapy training, Fauth and colleagues (2007) make the excellent point that for training to have lasting effects, it "needs to be aligned with and embedded within the organizational/treatment culture" (p. 387). In my experience with psychodynamically oriented training programs, this often means dealing with supervisors' attitudes, values, and assumptions about briefer modes of intervention.

In one of the few follow-up studies dealing with the long-term effects of training, LaRue-Yalom and Levenson (2001) questioned 90 professionals who previously (on average, 9 years ago) learned TLDP during their 6-month outpatient rotation at a large medical center. Results indicate that these professionals still used TLDP almost a decade later and reported that they called upon aspects of their TLDP training in their daily work. Of particular interest is the finding that many respondents said they had integrated TLDP formulation and intervention strategies into their longer-term work as well.

## BRIEF THERAPY IS NOT FOR EVERYONE

As previously mentioned, some problems do not lend themselves to a brief dynamic intervention—for example, severe characterological issues and severe depression. Also, some practitioners are not well suited to the interactive, directive, and self-disclosing strategies of brief dynamic psychotherapy. The "very intense and deep work of brief therapy is very demanding for the therapist" (Rawson, 2005, p. 159). In addition, the therapeutic perspectives necessary for the best practice of short-term dynamic approaches (outlined in Chapter 1) may be too much of a leap for those therapists who hold different attitudes, such as the belief that change can only come through a lengthy process of working through (Bolter et al., 1990). Without appropriate training and attention to these "resistances," we have found that asking such therapists to practice brief interventions will likely put them in situations of high ambivalence and inauthenticity (Levenson & Davidovitz, 2000).

The brief therapist has to have a high tolerance for ambiguity and deferment of gratification (perhaps indefinitely). For the therapist who has to bask in the success of his or her clients, the practice of short-term therapy should be avoided. So often by the time therapy ends, the journey for the client has just begun. There are often not the dramatic changes for self-congratulatory feelings or effusive appreciation from clients. Finally, brief therapists need to be able to say "hello" and say "goodbye" frequently. This can be wearing emotionally, and one needs to have good self-care skills and support.

Having said all of this, doing brief therapy is extremely rewarding. The work combines an optimistic, pragmatic, results-oriented attitude with the experience of deep emotional connection. Seeing positive shifts in the sessions and hearing about changes clients have made years later are profoundly satisfying. On a personal level, in the 30 years I have been conducting brief therapy, I have been phenomenally enriched, changed, and moved in countless small and dramatic ways by the power of being let into someone's life, albeit for a short stay.

In the next chapter I will discuss some of the ways brief dynamic therapy may change in the future, with my suggestions for developments in the field.

# Future Developments

I have divided my suggestions for future developments in brief dynamic therapy into three main areas having to do with clinical practice, research, and training.

## CLINICAL PRACTICE

*Practice from an Integrative Framework.* To a large extent this is already happening. Therapists are assimilating a variety of techniques into their "home" theory and are incorporating ideas from other theoretical orientations and other disciplines. For example, psychodynamically oriented brief therapists are attending workshops on neuroscience, listening to ethnologists, and learning how to use mindful meditation with clients. I am not suggesting that we all end up practicing from some grand integrative framework, but that we continue to engage in a lot of cross-talk.

*Continue the focus on positive affects and seeing the essence of our work as more than the removal of pain.* Psychodynamic therapists have been steeped in a pathological model for a very long time. Now brief dynamic therapists are in an ideal position—philosophically and procedurally—to focus on the power of joy, optimism, and growth.

*Abandon unrealistic, perfectionistic treatment goals and notions of "cure."* Instead we need to focus on reasonable yet meaningful change with the expectation that clients will return to therapy several times over their life span.

*Assume that clients can profit from a time-efficient point of view,* rather than expending effort on selecting the "just right" brief therapy candidate based on variables that are conceptually vague and hard to measure. But be ready to recognize as the therapy proceeds, there will be clients (and therapists!) who are not well suited to short-term interventions.

*Stay realistic and resist claiming we can do more and more with less and less.* The role of managed care companies in limiting the number of sessions and/or types of problems for bottom-line financial considerations has had a deleterious effect on the practice of psychotherapy in general, and on brief dynamic therapy in particular. We need to be careful that our outcome research (that demonstrates that change can occur quickly under the right circumstances) is not used by insurance providers to justify fewer and fewer sessions. Within some health maintenance organizations, therapies are so brief that there is insufficient time to allow processes such as forming an alliance, expressing emotions, and an unfolding of relational themes to occur.

*Focus on understanding the role of culture and diversity.* Culture is not something to be considered only for "minorities." Taking worldviews into account (especially as they affect the power dynamics within treatment) needs to be acknowledged as an integral part of our formulation and intervention strategies.

*Do not reify the concepts being investigated in developmental neuroscience.* While research in this area is burgeoning (and fascinating), clinicians, especially those with little neuroscience background, need to be careful not to jump to conclusions that we can identify specific neurological processes and brain structures to explain precisely why and how our therapeutic interventions work. Some therapists might be too ready to seize prematurely upon such objective findings. Nonetheless, the implications from work in this area (e.g., the human brain's plasticity for change) is reassuring, inspiring, and promising. And as stated by Siegel (2007) in his book on the *Mindful Brain,*

> at the very least, these discoveries confirmed a clinician's intuition that relationships are fundamental in a person's life and well-being. . . . [T]hese findings also verified the importance for each of us to be attuned to our own internal states in order to attune to others. (p. 168)

## RESEARCH

*Move away from an emphasis on "empirically supported therapies."* Some of the latest studies on brief dynamic therapy seem to be importing methodologies and perspectives from cognitive–behavioral research—looking for specified treatments for specific diagnoses. Research on brief therapy as practiced (rather than solely on controlled trials with carefully selected clients) should be applauded—and funded. Empirical investigation of intervention strategies and theories of change that therapists can use to inform their clinical work are needed (Westen, Novotny, & Thompson-Brenner, 2004). In fact, anything that encourages clinicians and researchers to carry on meaningful conversations should be promoted (Talley, Strupp, & Butler, 1994).

*Investigate the role of multicultural factors in brief therapy.* Brief dynamic therapy, as with all therapies, stands to gain a lot from learning more about cultural influences on the process of therapy; this will help us better serve the great numbers of people from diverse backgrounds who seek help.

*Encourage psychodynamically oriented brief therapists to find a way to do "mini-research" studies within their own agencies and practices.* Clinicians can use their own private practices to assess psychotherapy process and outcome data for their clients. And unlike rigorously controlled studies, therapists can use what they find in an ongoing way to make midcourse corrections. For some concrete suggestions on how to go about such mini-studies, see Levenson (1999).

*Investigate how best to teach brief dynamic principles to therapists and trainees.* The need for brief interventions will only grow. We need to learn how to best inform a new generation of practitioners to practice competently in a time-effective manner. The paucity of empirical work in this area is astounding given the enormous amount of time and effort devoted to teaching and supervision in most clinical programs. Having said this, there are some preliminary guidelines which I present in the following section.

## TRAINING

*Use manuals as a starting point.* It is my experience (and research confirms) that brief dynamic therapy training manuals provide a very useful beginning place for learning short-term approaches for those with little experience in the field. However, rigid adherence to such manuals should clearly be discouraged.

*Train brief dynamic therapists (regardless of the level of experience of the learner) with close, directive, and specific feedback.* Hands-on, guided practice is necessary. The use of video is invaluable in this regard. In fact, in my brief therapy training program, I rely on video to illustrate didactic points, and I supervise only if supervisees have taped their sessions and can show me portions of their recorded work for consultation.

My preferred teaching format is to present video segments of actual therapy sessions to small groups of trainees over an extended period of time, usually 6 months. The trainees in these seminars watch segments of sessions edited for specific training purposes (e.g., a segment involving a countertransferential reenactment). At predetermined places, I stop the video and ask the trainees to say what is going on, to distinguish between relevant and irrelevant material, to propose interventions the therapist might use, to justify their choices, and to anticipate the moment-to-moment behavior of the clients. The approach I am advocating is consistent with the teaching format of "anchored instruction," in which the knowledge to be learned is specifically tied to a particular problem using active involvement of the learner in a context that is highly similar to actual conditions (Binder, 2004; Schacht, 1991). For more information on the use of video for instructional purposes, see Levenson (1995).

*Focus on therapists' relational skills.* It is necessary to help brief therapy practitioners hone their abilities to recognize and track emotion accurately and empathically attune to clients. To what extent such skills can be learned remains an empirical question. Some training materials (e.g., Ekman, 2003) are designed to teach micro emotional recognition skills, but more procedural instructional materials are badly needed.

## SUMMARY

Brief dynamic therapy began as an effort to help clients as effectively and efficiently as possible, and pioneers in this area confronted many psychoanalytic taboos to do so. There have been many advances in the theory, research, and practice of brief dynamic therapy since then. The emphasis on the relational paradigm has been extremely helpful for refocusing what goes on in therapy from "there-and-then" to "here-and-now." This immediacy allows the therapeutic work to proceed in a much more enlivened, real-time way, promoting accelerated change. The refocusing from cognitive insight to affect has been another major paradigm shift that has allowed brief dynamic therapy to keep pace with current research and has again permitted more dramatic shifts inside and outside the therapy room. Concomitant with therapists' "rediscovery" of attachment theory and the central role of empathy, there has been a growth in research and clinical publications on the topic. The sizable empirical literature has settled once and for all, that brief therapy works; now we can move onto more clinically relevant topics such as why and for whom, by whom, and under what circumstances.

It is an exciting time to be learning and practicing in this field. The force of our interventions is substantial. We are pushing the limits of what is possible, and our clients are seeking out such treatments from a more knowledgeable place than ever before. My hope is that this book has provided an introduction to this fascinating topic and a starting point from which to explore the varieties and promise of brief dynamic psychotherapy.

# Glossary of Key Terms

CORE AFFECTIVE EXPERIENCES   Fosha (2000) defines these as one's emotional responses "when we do not try to mask, block, distort, or severely mute them" (p. 15).

CORRECTIVE EMOTIONAL EXPERIENCES   Alexander and French's (1946) original definition framed it as reexperiencing an old, unsettled conflict but with a "new ending." More recent definitions emphasize the relational aspects of experiencing the therapeutic relationship in a way that is different (e.g., healthier, more secure) and not expected given one's previous (dysfunctional) relational experiences.

COUNTERTRANSFERENCE   Classic countertransference, sometimes called *subjective countertransference*, "refers to the defensive and irrational reactions and feelings a therapist experiences with a particular patient" (Kiesler, 1996, p. 230) that are a product of that therapist's own unresolved conflicts or personality patterns. Interactive countertransference, also referred to as *objective countertransference*, "refers to the constricted feelings, attitudes, and reactions of a therapist, that are induced primarily by the patient's behavior and that are generalizable to other therapists" interacting with the same person (p. 230).

EMOTION-FOCUSED PSYCHOTHERAPY   An approach to individual, couples, and family therapy emphasizing the central role of emotion for understanding patterns of interaction and as a powerful change agent.

FELT SENSE   Term coined by Gendlin (1981) to refer to a vague, holistic, unconscious, preverbal sense of "something" experienced as an awareness in the body (versus symbolic or explicit ways of knowing).

IMMEDIACY   Disclosure within the therapy session of how the therapist is feeling about the client, about himself or herself in relation to the client, or about the therapy relationship (Hill, 2004); see metacommunication.

INTERPERSONAL NEUROBIOLOGY   An interdisciplinary approach combining what we know about the mind (which is seen as emerging from the interface of neurobiological and interpersonal processes) and what contributes to mental well-being (Siegel, 2006, p. 248); also known as *relational neuroscience*. It "assumes that the brain is a social organ that is built through experience" (Cosolino, 2006, p. 7).

MANAGED CARE   A health care delivery system designed to control costs and utilization while providing services. Insurance companies pay for or reimburse the cost of therapy and "managers," instead of clinicians, may get to decide how long the treatments should be and what types of problems may be treated, leading some to call it "managed cost" and even "mangled care."

MENTALIZING   A term used by Fonagy and Target (2006) to describe a psychological capacity of perceiving and interpreting human behavior in terms of intentional mental states (e.g., needs, feelings, motivations) of oneself and others.

METACOMMUNICATION   A process of talking about what is transpiring verbally and/or nonverbally between therapist and client.

SECURE BASE   A central concept in Bowlby's writings on parenting— "the provision by both parents of a secure base from which a child or an adolescent can make sorties into the outside world and to which he can return knowing for sure that he will be welcomed when he gets there, nourished physically and emotionally, comforted if distressed, reassured if frightened" (Bowlby, 1988, p. 11).

TIME-ATTENTIVE   Referring to an attitude on the therapist's part that indicates he or she is aware of time as a (usually limiting) factor in the therapeutic work.

# Suggested Readings

To learn more about various models of brief dynamic psychotherapy in general, the books by Messer and Warren (1995) and Levenson, Butler, Powers, and Beitman (2002) are good starting places. Karen (1998) has written a very accessible text on attachment that has value for both the neophyte and experienced practitioner. For therapists or trainees who want more fundamentals regarding process–experiential work, *Facilitating Emotional Change: The Moment-by-Moment Process* (Greenberg, Rice, & Elliott, 1993) is an excellent place to start. Cosolino's (2006) approach to the intriguing and developing field of interpersonal neurobiology has much to offer the clinician. *Psychotherapy Relationships That Work* (Norcross, 2002) describes understanding how improving the relationship between client and therapist leads to better outcomes rather than focusing on theory-driven techniques.

To explore time-limited dynamic psychotherapy (TLDP) further, there are three major texts (Binder, 2004; Levenson, 1995; Strupp & Binder, 1984). In addition, an entire chapter on TLDP formulation (Levenson & Strupp, 2007) can be found in Eells's *Handbook of Psychotherapy Case Formulation*. For a taste of how the here-and-now processes used in TLDP would work with couples and in groups, the reader is referred to *Creating Connection* (Johnson, 2004) and *The Theory and Practice of Group Psychotherapy* (Yalom, 1995). And of course, reading the original works by those who would become the early pioneers in brief dynamic therapy is a fascinating treat (e.g., Freud, Rank, Alexander).

For those readers with a cognitive–behaviorial orientation, I highly recommend Safran and Segal's book on interpersonal process in cognitive therapy.

For someone wanting to be exposed to what a session of brief dynamic psychotherapy looks and sounds like, there are several helpful videos (American Psychological Association; see http://www.apa.org/videos) that demonstrate such work with clients. In addition to reading and watching videos, I also recommend attending workshops in various models of dynamically oriented brief therapy that are given nationally and internationally.

The next step to learning is experiential. Try recording your own therapy sessions in audio or (preferably) video. As I tell my trainees, if they do nothing else than view their own work on tape, they will learn an incredible amount. As you watch or listen to your recorded sessions, use the CMP schematic (Figure 1, Chapter 4) to organize client information. And follow the formulation and intervention strategies outlined in Tables 4.1 and 4.2 as a guide. By using these items as a checklist, you can serve as your own rater to assess the degree to which you are doing TLDP. Having given all of these suggestions, there is nothing that surpasses ongoing clinical supervision (with a consultant who knows how to give *specific feedback* using recorded material within the context of a supervisory relationship). With such detailed feedback and the experience of a helpful relationship, one can begin to learn how to apply theoretical concepts and clinical strategies in real case situations.

Finally, our own clients are marvelous teachers. I can remember in one of my first clinical practica, I was feeling chagrined when a supervisor pointed out that I was missing something the client (a child) was telling me. She wisely told me, however, that the child would repeatedly try to convey what was important and that I would be successful if I could be open to hearing it. I think TLDP is one such thoughtful way to stay open.

## RECOMMENDED READINGS

Binder, J. L. (2004). *Key competencies in brief dynamic psychotherapy: Clinical practice beyond the manual.* New York, NY: Guilford Press.

Cosolino, L. (2006). *The neuroscience of human relationships: Attachments and the developing brain.* New York, NY: Norton.

Johnson, S. (2004). *Creating connection: The practice of emotionally focused couples therapy* (2nd ed.). New York, NY: Brunner-Routledge.

Karen, R. (1998). *Becoming attached: First relationships and how they shape our capacity to love.* New York, NY: Oxford University Press.

Levenson, H. (1995). *Time-limited dynamic psychotherapy: A guide to clinical practice.* New York, NY: Basic Books.

Levenson, H., Butler, S. F., Powers, T. A., & Beitman, B. (2002). *Concise guide to brief dynamic and interpersonal therapy.* Washington, DC: American Psychiatric Press.

Levenson, H., & Strupp, H. H. (2007). Cyclical maladaptive patterns: Case formulation in time-limited dynamic psychotherapy. In T. D. Eells (Ed.), *Handbook of psychotherapy case formulation* (2nd ed., pp. 164–197). New York, NY: Guilford Press.

Messer, S. B., & Warren, C. S. (1995). *Models of brief psychodynamic therapy: A comparative approach.* New York, NY: Guilford Press.

Norcross, J. C. (Ed.). (2002). *Psychotherapy relationships that work.* New York, NY: Oxford University Press.

Safran, J. D., & Segal, Z. V. (1990). *Interpersonal process in cognitive therapy.* New York, NY: Basic Books.

Strupp, H. H., & Binder, J. L. (1984). *Psychotherapy in a new key: A guide to time-limited dynamic psychotherapy.* New York, NY: Basic Books.

Yalom, I. D. (1995). *The theory and practice of group psychotherapy* (4th ed.). New York, NY: Basic Books.

# References

Abbass, A., Sheldon, A., Gyra, J., & Kalpin, A. (2008). Intensive short-term dynamic psychotherapy for DSM-IV personality disorders: A randomized controlled trial. *Journal of Nervous and Mental Disease, 196,* 211–216.

Adamson, O. L. B., & Frick, J. E. (2003). The still face: A history of a shared experimental paradigm. *Infancy, 4,* 451–473.

Ainsworth, M. D. S. (1967). *Infancy in Uganda: Infant care and the growth of love.* Baltimore, MD: Johns Hopkins University Press.

Ainsworth, M. D. S. (1969). Object relations, dependency and attachment: A theoretical review of the infant-mother relationship. *Child Development, 40,* 969–1025.

Ainsworth, M. D. S. (1989). Attachments beyond infancy. *American Psychologist, 44,* 709–716.

Alexander, F., & French, T. (1946). *Psychoanalytic therapy: Principles and applications.* New York, NY: Ronald Press.

Allen, J. G., Fonagy, P., & Bateman, A. W. (2008). *Mentalizing in clinical practice.* Washington, DC: American Psychiatric Press.

Altman, N. (1993). Psychoanalysis and the urban poor. *Psychoanalytic Dialogues, 3,* 29–50.

Anchin, J. C., & Kiesler, D. J. (Eds.). (1982). *Handbook of interpersonal psychotherapy.* New York, NY: Pergamon.

Anderson, E. M., & Lambert, M. J. (1995). Short-term dynamically oriented psychotherapy: A review and meta-analysis. *Clinical Psychology Review, 15,* 503–514.

Aron, L. (1991). The patient's experience of the analyst's subjectivity. *Psychoanalytic Dialogues, 11,* 29–51.

Aron, L. (1996). *A meeting of minds: Mutuality in psychoanalysis.* Hillsdale, NJ: Analytic Press.

Barber, J. P. (1994). Efficacy of short-term dynamic psychotherapy: Past, present, and future. *Journal of Psychotherapy Practice and Research, 3,* 108–121.

Barkham, M., Shapiro, D. A., Hardy, G. E., & Rees, A. (1999). Psychotherapy in two-plus-one sessions: Outcomes of a randomised controlled trial of cognitive–behavioral and psychodynamic–interpersonal therapy. *Journal of Consulting and Clinical Psychology, 67*, 201–211.

Barlow, D. H. (2000). Unraveling the mysteries of anxiety and its disorders from the perspective of emotion theory. *American Psychologist, 55*, 1247–1263.

Bauer, G. P., & Kobos, J. C. (1987). *Brief therapy: Short-term psychodynamic intervention.* Northdale, NJ: Jason Aronson.

Bauer, P. J. (1996). What do infants recall of their lives? Memory for specific events by one- to two-year olds. *American Journal of Psychology, 51*, 29–41.

Baxter, L. R., Schwartz, J. M., Bergman, K. S., Szuba, M. P., Guze, B. H., & Mazziotta, J. C. (1992). Caudate glucose metabolic rate changes with both drug and behavior therapy for obsessive-compulsive disorder. *Archives of General Psychiatry, 49,* 681–689.

Bedics, J. D., Henry, W. P., & Atkins, D. C. (2005). The therapeutic process as a predictor of change in patients' important relationships during time-limited dynamic psychotherapy. *Psychotherapy: Theory, Research, Practice, Training, 42,* 279–284.

Beebe, B., & Lachman, R. (1988). The contribution of mother–infant mutual influence to the origins of self and object representations. *Psychoanalytic Psychology, 5,* 305–357.

Bein, E., Anderson, T., Strupp, H. H., Henry, W. P., Schacht, T. E., Binder, J. L., & Butler, S. F. (2000). The effects of training in time-limited dynamic psychotherapy: Changes in therapeutic outcome. *Psychotherapy Research, 10,* 119–132.

Bein, E., Levenson, H., & Overstreet, D. (1994, June). Outcome and follow-up data from the VAST project. In H. Levenson (Chair), Outcome and Follow-up Data in Brief Dynamic Therapy. Symposium conducted at the annual international meeting of the Society for Psychotherapy Research, York, England.

Benjamin, L. S. (1974). Structural analysis of social behavior. *Psychological Review, 81,* 392–425.

Benjamin, L. S. (1993). *Interpersonal diagnosis and treatment of personality disorders.* New York, NY: Guilford Press.

Binder, J. L. (2004). *Key competencies in brief dynamic psychotherapy.* New York, NY: Guilford Press.

Bischoff, M. M., & Tracey, T. (1995). Client resistance as predicted by therapist behavior: A study of sequential dependence. *Journal of Counseling Psychology, 42,* 487–495.

Bollas, C. (1987). *The shadow of the object: Psychoanalysis of the unthought known.* New York, NY: Columbia University Press.

Bolter, K., Levenson, H., & Alvarez, W. (1990). Differences in values between short-term and long-term therapists. *Professional Psychology: Research and Practice, 21,* 285–290.

Book, H. E. (1998). *How to practice brief dynamic psychotherapy.* Washington, DC: American Psychological Association.

Boswell, J. F., & Castonguay, L. G. (2007). Guest editors introduction to special section on psychotherapy training. *Psychotherapy: Theory, Research, Practice, Training, 44,* 363.

Bowlby, J. (1969). *Attachment and loss: Vol. 1. Attachment.* New York, NY: Basic Books.

Bowlby, J. (1973). *Attachment and loss: Vol. 2. Separation anxiety and anger.* New York, NY: Basic Books.

Bowlby, J. (1980). *Attachment and loss: Vol.3. Loss, sadness, and depression.* New York, NY: Basic Books.

Bowlby, J. (1988). *A secure base: Clinical applications of attachment theory.* London, England: Routledge.

Bridges, M. R. (2006). Activating the corrective emotional experience. *Journal of Clinical Psychology: In Session, 62,* 551–568.

Budman, S. H., & Gurman, A. S. (1988). *Theory and practice of brief psychotherapy.* New York, NY: Guilford Press.

Burgoon, J. K. (1985). Nonverbal signals. In M. L. Knapp & G. R. Miller (Eds.), *Handbook of interpersonal communication* (pp. 344–390). Beverly Hills, CA: Sage Publications.

Burke, J. D. Jr., White, H. S., & Havens, L. L. (1979). Which short-term therapy? Matching patient and method. *Archives of General Psychiatry, 36,* 177–186.

Burke, W. (1992). Countertransference disclosure and the asymmetry/mutuality dilemma. *Psychoanalytic Dialogues, 2,* 241–271.

Burum, B. A., & Goldfried, M. R. (2007) The centrality of emotion to psychological change. *Clinical Psychology: Science and Practice, 14,* 407–413.

Butler, S. F., & Binder, J. L. (1987). Cyclical psychodynamics and the triangle of insight: An integration. *Psychiatry, 50,* 218–231.

Butler, S. F., & Strupp, H. H. (1988). The role of affect in time-limited dynamic psychotherapy. In S. H. Budman, & A. S. Gurman (Eds.), *Theory and practice of brief psychotherapy* (pp. 83–112). New York, NY: Guilford Press.

Butler, S. F., & the Center for Psychotherapy Research Team. (1986). *Working manual for the Vanderbilt Therapeutic Strategies Scale*. Unpublished manuscript, Vanderbilt University, Nashville, TN.

Butler, S. F., & Strupp, H. H. (1986). "Specific" and "nonspecific" factors in psychotherapy: A problematic paradigm for psychotherapy research. *Psychotherapy: Theory, Research and Practice, 23*, 30–40.

Butler, S. F., & Strupp, H. H. (1989, June). *Issues in training therapists to competency: The Vanderbilt experience*. Paper presented at the annual meeting of the Society for Psychotherapy Research, Toronto, Ontario, Canada.

Butler, S. F., Strupp, H. H., & Binder, J. L. (1993). Time-limited dynamic psychotherapy. In S. Budman, M. Hoyt, & S. Friedman (Eds.), *The first session in brief therapy*. New York, NY: Guilford Press.

Butler, S. F., Thackrey, M., & Strupp, H. H. (1987, June). Capacity for Dynamic Process Scale (CDPS): Relation to patient variables, process and outcome. Paper presented at the annual meeting of the Society for Psychotherapy Research, Ulm, West Germany.

Butler, S. F., Flasher, L. V., & Strupp, H. H. (1993). Countertransference and qualities of the psychotherapist. In N. E. Miller, L. Luborsky, J. P. Barber, & J. P. Docherty (Eds.), *Psychodynamic treatment research: A handbook for clinical practice*. New York, NY: Basic Books.

Cameron, C. L. (2006). Brief psychotherapy: A brief review. *American Journal of Psychotherapy, 60*, 147–152.

Castonguay, L. G., & Beutler, L. E. (2005). *Principles of therapeutic change that work*. New York, NY: Oxford University Press.

Castonguay, L. G., & Hill, C. E. (Eds.). (2007). *Insight in psychotherapy*. Washington, DC: American Psychological Association.

Chiron, C., Jambaque, I., Nabbout, R., Lounes, R., Syrotam, A., & Dulac, O. (1997). The right brain is dominant in human infants. *Brain, 120*, 1057–1065.

Chrzanowski, G. (1982). Interpersonal formulations of psychotherapy. In J. D. Anchin & D. J. Kiesler (Eds.), *Handbook of interpersonal psychotherapy* (pp. 25–45). New York, NY: Pergamon Press.

Connolly, M. B., Crits-Christoph, P., Demorest, A., Azarian, K., Muenz, L., & Chittams, I. (1996). Varieties of transference patterns in psychotherapy. *Journal of Consulting and Consulting Psychology, 64*, 1213–1221.

Cooley, C. H. (1902). *Human nature and the social order.* New York, NY: Scribner.

Cooper, S. H. (1987). Changes in psychoanalytic ideas: Transference interpretations. *Journal of the American Psychoanalytic Association, 35*, 77–98.

Cosolino, L. (2006). *The neuroscience of human relationships: Attachments and the developing brain.* New York, NY: Norton.

Crits-Christoph, P. (1992). The efficacy of brief dynamic psychotherapy: A meta-analysis. *American Journal of Psychiatry, 149*, 151–158.

Crits-Christoph, P., Barber, J. P., & Kurcias, J. S. (1991). Introduction and historical background. In P. Crits-Christoph & J. P. Barber (Eds.), *Handbook of short-term dynamic psychotherapy* (pp. 1–12). New York, NY: Basic Books.

Cummings, N. A. (1986). The dismantling of our health system: Strategies for the survival of psychological practice. *American Psychologist, 41*, 426–431.

Cummings, N. A. (1995). Unconscious fiscal convenience. *Psychotherapy in Private Practice, 14*, 23–28.

Damasio, A. (1999). *The feeling of what happens.* New York, NY: Harcourt, Brace.

Davanloo, H. (Ed.). (1978). *Basic principles and techniques in short-term dynamic psychotherapy.* New York, NY: Spectrum.

Davanloo, H. (1986). Intensive short-term psychotherapy with highly resistant patients, I: Handling resistance. *International Journal of Short-Term Psychotherapy, 1*, 107–133.

DeMaat, S., Dekker, J., Schoevers, R., vanAalst, G., Gijsbers-vanWijk, C., Henriksen, M., et al. (2008). Short psychodynamic supportive psychotherapy, antidepressants and their combination in the treatment of major depression: A mega-analysis based on three randomized clinical trials. *Depression and Anxiety, 25*, 565–574.

Diener, M. C., Hilsenroth, M. J., & Weinberger, J. (2007). Therapist affect, focus and patient outcomes in psychodynamic psychotherapy: A meta-analysis. *American Journal of Psychiatry, 164*, 936–941.

Eagle, M. N. (1984). *Recent developments in psychoanalysis: A critical evaluation.* New York, NY: McGraw-Hill.

Ekman, P. (2003). *Emotions revealed.* New York, NY: Holt.

Ekman, P., & Davidson, R. J. (1994). *The nature of emotion: Fundamental questions.* New York, NY: Oxford University Press.

Ekman, P., & Friesen, W. V. (1969). The repertoire of nonverbal behavior: Categories origins, usage, and coding. *Semiotica, 1,* 49–98.

Elliott, R. (2001). Contemporary brief experiential psychotherapy. *Clinical Psychology: Science and Practice, 8,* 38–50.

Emde, R. N. (1991). Positive emotions for psychoanalytic theory: Surprises from infancy research and new directions. *Journal of the American Psychoanalytic Association, 39,* 5–44.

Ezriel, H. (1950). A psychoanalytic approach to group treatment. *British Journal of Medical Psychology, 23,* 59–74.

Fauth, J., Gates, S., Vinca, M. A., Boles, S., & Hayes, J. A. (2007). Big ideas for psychotherapy training. *Psychotherapy: Theory, Research, Practice, Training, 44,* 384–391.

Fauth, J., Smith, S., & Mathisen, A. (2005, June). *A naturalistic study of the effectiveness of training in time limited dynamic psychotherapy for clinical psychology trainees.* Paper presented at the international meeting of the Society for Psychotherapy Research, Montreal, Quebec, Canada.

Fenichel, O. (1941). *Problems of psychoanalytic technique.* New York, NY: Psychoanalytic Quarterly.

Ferenczi, S. (1920/1950). Technical difficulties in the analysis of a case of hysteria. In J. Rickman (Ed.), *Further contributions to the theory and technique of psychoanalysis.* London, England: Hogarth.

Ferenczi, S., & Rank, O. (1925). *The development of psychoanalysis.* New York, NY: Nervous and Mental Disease Publication.

Flegenheimer, W. V. (1982). *Techniques of brief psychotherapy.* New York, NY: Aronson.

Florsheim, P., Henry, W. P., & Benjamin, L. S. (1996). Integrating individual and interpersonal approach to diagnosis. In F. W. Kaslow (Ed.), *Handbook of relational diagnosis and dysfunctional family patterns* (pp. 81–101). New York, NY: Wiley.

Fonagy, P., Gergely, G., Jurist, E. L., & Target, M. (2002). *Affect regulation, mentalization, and the development of the self.* New York, NY: Other Press.

Fonagy, P., Roth, A., & Higgitt, A. (2005). Psychodynamic psychotherapies: Evidenced-based practice and clinical wisdom. *Bulletin of the Menninger Clinic, 69,* 1–58.

Fonagy, P., & Target, M. (2006). The mentalization focused approach to self psychology. *Journal of Personality Disorders, 20,* 544–576.

Fosha, D. (1995). Technique and taboo in three short-term dynamic psychotherapies. *Journal of Psychotherapy Practice and Research, 4,* 297–318.

Fosha, D. (2000). *The transforming power of affect: A model for accelerated change.* New York, NY: Basic Books.

Fosha, D. (2003). Dyadic regulation and experiential work with emotion and relatedness in trauma and disorganized attachment. In M. F. Solomon & D. J. Siegel (Eds.), *Healing trauma: Attachment, mind, body, and brain* (pp. 221–281). New York, NY: Norton.

Frank, J. D., & Frank, J. B. (1991). *Persuasion and healing: A comparative study of psychotherapy* (3rd ed.). Baltimore, MD: Johns Hopkins University Press.

Fredrickson, B. (2001). The role of positive emotions in positive psychology: The broaden and build theory of positive emotions. *American Psychologist, 56,* 218–226.

Freud, S. (1904/1953). Psycho-analytic method. In E. Jones (Ed.) & J. Riviere (Trans.), *Collected papers of Sigmund Freud: Early papers, Vol 1* (pp. 264–271). London, England: Hogarth Press.

Freud, S. (1909/2004). *An introduction to psychoanalysis.* New York, NY: Kessinger.

Freud, S. (1912/1924). Recommendations for physicians on the psycho-analytic method of treatment. In E. Jones (Ed.) & J. Riviere (Trans.), *Collected papers of Sigmund Freud, Vol 2.* (pp. 323–333). London, England: Hogarth Press.

Freud, S. (1933/1964). New introductory lectures on psycho-analysis. *Standard Edition, Vol. 22* (pp. 2–128). London, England: Hogarth Press.

Freud, S. (1937/1964). Analysis terminable and interminable. *Standard Edition, Vol. 23* (pp. 209–253). London, England: Hogarth Press.

Frewen, P. A., Dozois, D., & Lanius, R. A. (2008). Neuroimaging studies of psychological interventions for mood and anxiety disorders: Empirical and methodological review. *Clinical Psychology Review, 28,* 229–247.

Frijda, N. H. (1986). *The emotions.* Cambridge, England: Cambridge University Press.

Gabbard, G. O. (1993). An overview of countertransference with borderline patients. *Journal of Psychotherapy Practice and Research, 2,* 7–18.

Gallese, V. (2003). The roots of empathy: The shared manifold hypothesis and the neural basis of intersubjectivity. *Psychopathology, 36,* 171–180.

Garfield, S. L. (1994). Research on client variables in psychotherapy. In A. E. Bergin & S. L. Garfield (Eds.), *Handbook of psychotherapy and behavior change* (4th ed., pp. 190–228). New York, NY: Wiley.

Gelso, C. J. (2004). Countertransference and its management in brief dynamic therapy. In D. P. Charman (Ed.), *Core processes in brief psychodynamic psychotherapy* (pp. 231–250). Mahwah, NJ: Erlbaum.

Gendlin, E. T. (1981). *Focusing.* New York, NY: Bantam Books.

Gendlin, E. T. (1991). On emotion in therapy. In J. D. Safran & L. S. Greenberg (Eds.), *Emotions, psychotherapy, and change* (pp. 255–279). New York, NY: Guilford Press.

Gendlin, E. T. (1996). *Focusing-oriented psychotherapy: A manual of the experiential method.* New York, NY: Guilford Press.

Gibbons, M. B., Crits-Christoph, P., & Hearon, B. (2008). The empirical status of psychodynamic therapies. *Annual Review of Clinical Psychology, 4,* 93–108.

Gill, M. M. (1982). *Analysis of transference: Vol. 1. Theory and technique.* New York, NY: International Universities Press.

Gill, M. M. (1993). Interaction and interpretation. *Psychoanalytic Dialogues, 3,* 111–122.

Gleiser, K., Ford, J. D., & Fosha, D. (2008). Contrasting exposure and experiential therapies for complex posttraumatic stress disorder. *Psychotherapy: Theory, Research, Practice, Training, 45,* 340–360.

Goldapple, K., Segal, Z., Garson, C., Lau, M., Bieling, P., Kennedy, S., & Mayberg, H. (2004). Modulation of cortical-limbic pathways in major depression: Treatment-specific effects of cognitive behavior therapy. *Archives of General Psychiatry, 61,* 34–41.

Goleman, D. (1995). *Emotional intelligence.* New York, NY: Bantam Books.

Greenberg, J. R. (1991). Countertransference and reality. *Psychoanalytic Dialogues, 1,* 52–73.

Greenberg, L. S. (2002). *Emotion-focused therapy: Coaching clients to work through their feelings.* Washington, DC: American Psychological Association.

Greenberg, L. S. (2004). Emotion-focused therapy. *Clinical Psychology and Psychotherapy, 11,* 3–16.

Greenberg, L. S., & Johnson, S. (1988). *Emotionally focused therapy for couples.* New York, NY: Guilford Press.

Greenberg, L. S., & Paivio, S. C. (1997). *Working with the emotions in psychotherapy.* New York, NY: Guilford Press.

Greenberg, L. S., & Pascual-Leone, J. (2006). Emotion in psychotherapy: A practice-friendly research review. *Journal of Clinical Psychology: In Session, 62,* 611–630.

Greenberg, L.S., Rice, L. N., & Elliott, R. (1993). *Facilitating emotional change: The moment-by-moment process.* New York, NY: Guilford Press.

Greenberg, L. S., & Safran, J. D. (1987). *Emotion in psychotherapy: Affect, cognition, and the process of change.* New York, NY: Guilford Press.

Grotjahn, M. (1966). *Franz Alexander: Western mind in translation.* In F. Alexander, S. Eisenstein, & M. Grotjahn (Eds.), *Psychoanalytic pioneers.* New York, NY: Basic Books.

Hansen, N. B., & Lambert, M. J. (2003). An evaluation of the dose-response relationship in naturalistic treatment settings using survival analysis. *Mental Health Services Research, 5,* 1–12.

Hansen, N. B., Lambert, M. J., & Forman, E. M. (2002). The psychotherapy dose-response effect and its implications for treatment delivery services. *Clinical Psychology: Science and Practice, 9,* 329–343.

Harlow, H. F. (1959). Love in infant monkeys. *Scientific American, 200,* 68–86.

Hartmann, K., & Levenson, H. (1995, June). *Case formulation and countertransference in time-limited dynamic psychotherapy.* Presentation at the annual meeting of the Society for Psychotherapy Research, Vancouver, British Columbia, Canada.

Henry, W. P., Schacht, T. E., & Strupp, H. H. (1990). Patient and therapist introject, interpersonal process, and differential psychotherapy outcome. *Journal of Consulting and Clinical Psychology, 58,* 768–774.

Henry, W. P., Schacht, T. E., Strupp, H. H., Butler, S., & Binder, J. L. (1993a). Effects of training in time-limited dynamic psychotherapy: Mediators of therapists' responses to training. *Journal of Consulting and Clinical Psychology, 61,* 441–447.

Henry, W. P., Strupp, H. H., Butler, S. F., Schacht, T. E., & Binder, J. L. (1993b). Effects of training in time-limited dynamic psychotherapy: Changes in therapist behavior. *Journal of Consulting and Clinical Psychology, 61,* 434–440.

Hesse, E., Main, M., Abrams, K. Y., & Rifkin, A. (2003). Unresolved states regarding loss or abuse can have "second-generation" effects: Disorganization, role-inversion, and frightening ideation in the offspring of traumatized non-maltreating parents. In M. F. Solomon & D. J. Siegel (Eds.), *Healing trauma: Attachment, mind, body, brain* (pp. 57–106). New York, NY: Norton.

Hill, C. E. (2004). *Helping skills: Facilitating exploration, insight, and action* (2nd ed.). Washington, DC: American Psychological Association.

Hilliard, R. B., Henry, W. P., & Strupp, H. H. (2000). An interpersonal model of psychotherapy: Linking patient and therapist developmental history, therapeutic process, and types of outcome. *Journal of Consulting and Clinical Psychology, 68,* 125–133.

Hilsenroth, M. J. (2007). A programmatic study of short-term psychodynamic psychotherapy: Process, outcome, and training. *Psychotherapy Research, 17,* 31–45.

Hilsenroth, M. J., Ackerman, S., & Blagys, M. (2001). Evaluating phase models of change during short-term dynamic psychotherapy. *Psychotherapy Research, 11,* 29–47.

Hilsenroth, M. J., Defife, J. A., Blagys, M. D., & Ackerman, S. J. (2006). Effects of training in short-term psychodynamic psychotherapy: Changes in graduate clinician technique. *Psychotherapy Research, 16,* 293–305.

Hirsch, I. (1992). An interpersonal perspective: The analyst's unwitting participating in the patient's change. *Psychotherapy, 26,* 290–295.

Hobbs, M. (2006). Short-term dynamic psychotherapy. In S. Block (Ed.), *Introduction to the Psychotherapies* (4th ed.). Melbourne, Australia: Oxford University Press.

Hoffman, I. Z. (1992). Some practical implications of a social-constructivist view of the psychoanalytic situation. *Psychoanalytic Dialogues, 2,* 287–304.

Hoglend, P. (2003). Long-term effects of brief dynamic psychotherapy. *Psychotherapy Research, 13,* 271–292.

Hoglend, P., Johansson, P., Marble, A., Bogwald, K., & Amlo, S. (2007). Moderators of the effects of transference interpretations on brief dynamic psychotherapy. *Psychotherapy Research, 17,* 162–174.

Holmes, J. (1993). *John Bowlby and attachment theory.* London, England: Routledge.

Horowitz, M. J., Marmar, C. R., Weiss, D. S., et al. (1984). *Personality styles and brief psychotherapy.* New York, NY: Basic Books.

Horowitz, L., & Strack, S. (in press). *Handbook of interpersonal psychology.* New York, NY: Wiley.

Horowitz, L., & Vitkus, J. (1986). The interpersonal basis of psychiatric symptoms. *Clinical Psychology Review, 6,* 443–469.

Horvarth, A. O., & Greenberg, L. S. (1994). *The working alliance: Theory, research, and practice.* New York, NY: Wiley.

Howard, K. I., Kopta, S. M., Krause, M. S., & Orlinsky, D. E. (1986). The dose-effect relationship in psychotherapy. *American Psychologist, 41,* 159–164.

Howard, K. I., Leuger, R. S., Maling, M. S., & Martinovich, Z. (1993). A phase model of psychotherapy. *Journal of Consulting and Clinical Psychology, 61,* 678–685.

Howard, K. I., Moras, K., Brill, P., Martinovich, Z., & Lutz, N. (1996). Evaluation of psychotherapy: Efficacy, effectiveness, and patient progress. *American Psychologist, 51,* 1059–1064.

Hoyt, M. F. (1985). Therapist resistances to short-term dynamic psychotherapy. *Journal of the American Academy of Psychoanalysis, 13,* 93–112.

Hoyt, M. F., Rosenbaum, R., & Talmon, M. (1992). Planned single-session psycho-therapy. In S. Budman, M. F. Hoyt, & S. Friedman (Eds.), *The first session in brief therapy* (pp. 59–86). New York, NY: Guilford Press.

Iacoboni, M. (2008). *Mirroring people: The new science of how we connect to others.* New York, NY: Farrar, Straus, and Giroux.

Ivy, G. (2006). A method of teaching psychodynamic case formulation. *Psycho-therapy: Theory, Research, Practice, Training, 43,* 322–336.

James, W. (1890/1981). *Principles of psychology.* Cambridge, MA: Harvard University Press.

Johnson, M. E., Popp, C., Schacht, T. E., Mellon, J., & Strupp, H. H. (1989). Converg-ing evidence for identification of recurrent relationship themes: Comparison of two methods. *Psychiatry 52,* 275–288.

Johnson, S. (2004). *Creating connection: The practice of emotionally focused couples therapy* (2nd ed.). New York, NY: Brunner-Routledge.

Johnson, S., Bradley, B., Furrow, J., Lee, A., Palmer, G., Tilley, D., & Woolley, S. (2005). *Becoming an emotionally focused couple therapist: The workbook.* New York, NY: Brunner-Routledge.

Jones, E. (1955). *The life and work of Sigmund Freud, Vol. 2.* New York, NY: Basic Books.

Junkert-Tress, B., Schnierda, U., Hartkamp, N., Schmitz, N., & Tress, W. (2001). Effects of short-term dynamic psychotherapy for neurotic, somatoform, and personality disorders. *Psychotherapy Research, 11,* 187–200.

Jurist, E. L., & Meehan, K. B. (2008). Attachment, mentalization, and reflective func-tioning. In J. H. Obegi & E. Berant (Eds.), *Attachment theory and research in clinical work with adults* (pp. 71–93). New York, NY: Guilford Press.

Kadera, S. W., Lambert, M. J., & Andrews, A. A. (1996). How much therapy is really enough? *The Journal of Psychotherapy Practice and Research, 5,* 132–151.

Karen, R. (1998). *Becoming attached: First relationships and how they shape our capac-ity to love.* New York, NY: Oxford University Press.

Kasper, L. B., Hill, C. E., & Kivlighan, D. M. (2008). Therapist immediacy in brief psychotherapy: Case study I. *Psychotherapy Theory, Research, Practice, Training, 45,* 281–297.

Kelly, G. (1955). *Psychology of personal constructs.* New York, NY: Norton.

Kiesler, D. J. (1982). Confronting the client-therapist relationship in psychotherapy. In J. C. Anchin & D. J. Kiesler (Eds.), *Handbook of interpersonal psychotherapy* (pp. 274–295). New York, NY: Pergamon Press.

Kiesler, D. J. (1988). *Therapeutic metacommunication: Therapist impact disclosure as feedback in psychotherapy.* Palo Alto, CA: Consulting Psychologists Press.

Kiesler, D. J. (1991). Interpersonal methods of assessment and diagnosis. In C. R. Snyder & D. R. Forsyth (Eds.), *Handbook of social and clinical psychology* (pp. 438–468). Elmsford, NY: Pergamon Press.

Kiesler, D. J. (1996). *Contemporary interpersonal theory and research.* New York, NY: Wiley.

Kivligan, D. M., Jr. (1989). Changes in counselor intentions and response modes in client reactions and session evaluation after training. *Journal of Counseling Psychology, 36,* 471–476.

Kivligan, D. M., Jr., Angelone, E. O., & Swofford, K. (1991). Live supervision in individual counseling. *Professional Psychology: Research and Practice, 22,* 489–495.

Kivligan, D. M., Jr., Schuetz, S. A., & Kardash, C. M. (1998). Counselor trainee achievement: Goal orientation and the acquisition of time-limited dynamic psychotherapy skills. *Journal of Counseling Psychology, 45,* 189–195.

Knekt, P., Lindfors, O., Harkanen, T., Valikoski, M., Virtala, E., Laaksonen, M. A., et al. (2008). Randomized trial on the effectiveness of long-and short-term psychodynamic psychotherapy and solution-focused therapy on psychiatric symptoms during a three year follow up. *Psychological Medicine, 38,* 689–703.

Kohlenberg, R. J., & Tsai, M. (1991). *FAP: Functional analytic psychotherapy.* New York, NY: Plenum.

Kopta, S. M., Howard, K. I., Lowry, J. L., & Beutler, L. E. (1994). Patterns of symptomatic recovery in psychotherapy. *Journal of Consulting and Clinical Psychology, 62,* 1009–1016.

Koss, M., & Shiang, J. (1994). Research on brief psychotherapy. In A. Bergin & S. Garfield (Eds.), *Handbook of psychotherapy and behavior change (4th ed.).* New York, NY: Wiley.

Lambert, M. J., & Asay, T. P. (2004). Measuring clinically significant change. In D. P. Charman (Ed.), *Core processes in brief psychodynamic psychotherapy* (pp. 309–322). Mahwah, NJ: Erlbaum.

Lambert, M., Bergin, A., & S. Garfield (Eds.). (2004). *Handbook of psychotherapy and behavior change (5th ed.).* New York, NY: Wiley.

Lambert, M., Garfield, S., & Bergin, S. (2004). Overviews, trends and future issues. In M. Lambert, A. Bergin, & S. Garfield (Eds.), *Handbook of psychotherapy and behavior change (5th ed.).* New York, NY: Wiley.

LaRoche, M. J. (1999). Culture, transference, and countertransference among Latinos. *Psychotherapy, 36,* 389–397.

LaRue-Yalom, T., & Levenson, H. (2001, August). *Long-term outcome of training in time-limited dynamic psychotherapy.* Paper presented at the American Psychological Association Convention, San Francisco, CA.

Lazarus, R. S. (1991). *Emotion and adaptation.* New York, NY: Oxford University Press.

LeDoux, J. (1996). *The emotional brain: The mysterious underpinnings of emotional life.* New York, NY: Simon & Schuster.

Leichsenring, F., Rabung, S., & Leibing, E. (2004). The efficacy of short-term psychodynamic psychotherapy in specific psychiatric disorders: A meta-analysis. *Archives of General Psychiatry, 61,* 1208–1216.

Levenson, H. (1995). *Time-limited dynamic psychotherapy: A guide to clinical practice.* New York, NY: Basic Books.

Levenson, H. (1999). Psychotherapy research. *Psychotherapy Bulletin, 33,* 47–50.

Levenson, H. (2003). Time-limited dynamic psychotherapy: An integrationist perspective. *Journal of Psychotherapy Integration, 13,* 300–333.

Levenson, H., & Bein, E. (1993, June). *VA short-term psychotherapy research project: Outcome.* Paper presented at the annual meeting of the Society for Psychotherapy Research, Pittsburgh, PA.

Levenson, H., & Bolter, K. (1988, August). *Short-term psychotherapy values and attitudes: Changes with training.* Paper presented at the American Psychological Association Convention, Atlanta, GA.

Levenson, H., & Burg, J. (2000). Training psychologists in the era of managed care. In K. A. Hersen & M. Hersen (Eds.), *A psychologist's proactive guide to managed mental health care* (pp. 113–140). Hillsdale, NJ: Erlbaum.

Levenson, H., & Butler, S. (1994). Brief psychodynamic individual psychotherapy. In R. Hales & J. Talbot (Eds.), *Textbook of psychiatry* (pp. 1009–1033). Washington, DC: American Psychiatric Press.

Levenson, H., Butler, S., & Bein, E. (2002). Brief psychodynamic individual psychotherapy. In R. Hales, S. C. Yudofsky, & J. Talbot (Eds.), *American Psychiatric Press textbook of psychiatry* (pp. 1133–1156). Washington, DC: American Psychiatric Press.

Levenson, H., Butler, S., Powers, T., & Beitman, B. (2002). *Concise guide to brief dynamic and interpersonal psychotherapy.* Washington, DC: American Psychiatric Press.

Levenson, H., & Davidovitz, D. (2000). Brief therapy prevalence and training: A national survey of psychologists. *Psychotherapy, 37,* 335–340.

Levenson, H., & Evans, S. A. (2000). The current state of brief therapy training in American Psychological Association accredited graduate and internship programs. *Professional Psychology: Research and Practice, 31,* 446–452.

Levenson, H., & Overstreet, D. (1993, June). Long-term outcome with brief psychotherapy. Paper presented at the annual meeting of Society for Psychotherapy Research, Pittsburgh, PA.

Levenson, H., & Strupp, H. H. (1999). Recommendations for the future of training in brief dynamic psychotherapy. *Journal of Clinical Psychology, 55,* 385–391.

Levenson, H., & Strupp, H. H. (2007). Cyclical maladaptive patterns: Case formulation in time-limited dynamic psychotherapy. In T. D. Eells (Ed.), *Handbook of psychotherapy case formulation* (2nd ed., pp. 164–197). New York, NY: Guilford Press.

Lewis, T., Amini, F., & Lannon, R. (2001). *A general theory of love.* New York, NY: Vintage Books.

Linehan, M. M. (1993). *Cognitive–behavioral treatment of borderline personality disorder.* New York, NY: Guilford Press.

Lorenz, K. Z. (1957). *Instinctive behavior.* New York, NY: International Universities Press.

Luborsky, L. (1984). *Principles of psychoanalytic psychotherapy: A manual for supportive-expressive treatment.* New York, NY: Basic Books.

Luborsky, L., & Crits-Christoph, P. (1990). *Understanding transference: The CCRT method.* New York, NY: Basic Books.

MacKenzie, K. R. (1991). Principles of brief intensive psychotherapy. *Psychiatric Annals, 21,* 398–404.

Magnavita, J. J. (1997). *Restructuring personality disorders.* New York, NY: Guilford Press.

Magnavita, J. J. (2006). Emotion in short-term psychotherapy: An introduction. *Journal of Clinical Psychology: In Session, 62,* 517–522.

Magnavita, J. J. (2008). Psychoanalytic psychotherapy. In J. L. Lebow (Ed.), *Twenty-first century psychotherapies* (pp. 206–236). New York, NY: Wiley.

Main, M., Kaplan, N., & Cassidy, J. (1985). Security in infancy, childhood, and adulthood: A move to the level of representation. *Monographs of the Society for Research in Child Development, 50,* 66–104.

Malan, D. H. (1963). *A study of brief psychotherapy.* London, England: Tavistock.

Malan, D. H. (1976). *The frontier of brief psychotherapy.* New York, NY: Plenum.

Malan, D. H. (1980). The most important development in psychotherapy since the discovery of the unconscious. In J. Davanloo (Ed.), *Short-term dynamic psychotherapy.* New York, NY: Aronson.

Mann, J. (1973). *Time-limited psychotherapy.* Cambridge, MA: Harvard University Press.

Marmor, J. (1979). Short-term dynamic psychotherapy. *American Journal of Psychiatry, 136,*149–155.

Marsella, A. J., & Kameoka, V. A. (1989). Ethnocultural issues in the assessment of psychopathology. In S. Wetzler (Ed.), *Measuring mental illness: Psychometric assessment for clinicians* (pp. 231–256). Washington, DC: American Psychiatric Press.

Martin, D. J., Garske, J. P., & Davis, M. K. (2000). Relation of the therapeutic alliance with outcome and other variables: A meta-analytic review. *Journal of Consulting and Clinical Psychology, 68,* 438–450.

McCarthy, P. R., & Betz, N. E. (1978). Differential effects of self-disclosing versus self-involved counselor statements. *Journal of Counseling Psychology, 25,* 251–256.

McCullough, L., Kuhn, N., Andrews, S., Kaplan, A., Wolf, J., & Hurley, C. L. (2003). *Treating affect phobia: A manual for short-term dynamic psychotherapy.* New York, NY: Guilford Press.

McCullough Vaillant, L. (1997). *Changing character: Short-term anxiety-regulating psychotherapy for restructuring defenses, affects, and attachment.* New York, NY: Basic Books.

Meltzoff, A. N., & Moore, M. K. (1977). Imitation of facial and manual gestures by human neonates. *Science, 198,* 75–78.

Messer, S. B. (1992). A critical examination of belief structures in integrative and eclectic psychotherapy. In J. C. Norcross & M. R. Goldfried (Eds.), *Handbook of psychotherapy integration* (pp. 130–165). New York, NY: Basic Books.

Messer, S. B., & Kaplan, A. H. (2004). Outcomes and factors related to efficacy of brief psychodynamic therapy. In D. P. Charman (Ed.), *Core processes in brief psychodynamic psychotherapy* (pp. 103–118). Mahwah, NJ: Erlbaum.

Messer, S. B., & Warren, C. S. (1995). *Models of brief psychodynamic therapy: A comparative approach.* New York, NY: Guilford Press.

Mikulincer, M., & Shaver, P. R. (2007). *Attachment in adulthood: Structure, dynamics, and change.* New York, NY: Guilford Press.

Mitchell, S. (1988). *Relational concepts in psychoanalysis: An integration.* Cambridge, MA: Harvard University Press.

Multon, K. D., Kivlighan, D. M., & Gold, P. B. (1996). Changes in counselor adherence over the course of training. *Journal of Counseling Psychology, 43,* 356–363.

Muran, J. C. (2001). A final note: Meditations on "both/and." In J. C. Muran (Ed.), *Self-relations in the psychotherapy process* (pp. 347–372). Washington, DC: American Psychological Association.

Muran, J. C., Safran, J. D., Gorman, B. S., Samstag, L. W., Eubanks-Carter, C., & Winston, A. (2009). The relationship of early alliance ruptures to their resolution to process and outcome in three time-limited psychotherapies for personality disorders. *Psychotherapy: Theory, Research, Practice, Training, 46,* 233–248.

Neborsky, R. J. (2006). Brain, mind, and dyadic change processes. *Journal of Clinical Psychology: In Session, 62,* 523–538.

Neff, W. L., Lambert, M. J., Kirk, M. L., Lunnen, K. M., Budman, S. H., & Levenson, H. (1997). Therapists' attitudes toward short-term therapy: Changes with training. *Employee Assistance Quarterly 11,* 67–77.

Nielsen, G., & Barth, K. (1991). Short-term anxiety-provoking psychotherapy. In P. Crits-Christoph & J. P. Barber (Eds.), *Handbook of short-term dynamic psychotherapy.* New York, NY: Basic Books.

Norcross, J. C. (Ed.). (2002). *Psychotherapy relationships that work.* New York, NY: Oxford University Press.

Obegi, J. H., & Berant, E. (2008). Introduction. In J. H. Obegi & E. Berant (Eds.), *Attachment theory and research in clinical work with adults* (pp. 1–14). New York, NY: Guilford Press.

Ogden, T. (1982). *Projective identification and psychotherapeutic technique.* Northvale, NJ: Aronson.

Ogden, T. H. (1994). *Subjects of analysis.* Northvale, NJ: Aronson.

Olfson, M., & Pincus, H. A. (1994). Outpatient psychotherapy in the United States: II. Patterns of utilization. *American Journal of Psychiatry, 151,* 1289–1294.

Orlinsky, D. E., Gawe, K., & Parks, B. K. (1994). Process and outcome in psychotherapy: Noch einmal. In A. E. Bergin & S. L. Garfield (Eds.), *Handbook of psychotherapy and behavior change* (4th ed., pp. 270–376). New York, NY: Wiley.

Overstreet, D. L. (1993). *Patient contribution to differential outcome in time-limited dynamic psychotherapy: An empirical analysis.* Unpublished doctoral dissertation, Wright Institute, Berkeley, CA.

Panksepp, J. (1998). *Affective neuroscience: The foundations of human and animal emotions.* New York, NY: Oxford University Press.

Peake, T. H., Bordin, C. M., & Archer, R. P. (1988). *Brief psychotherapies: Changing frames of mind.* Beverly Hills, CA: Sage.

Pekarik, G., & Wierzbicki, M. (1986). The relationship between clients' expected and actual treatment duration. *Psychotherapy, 23,* 532–534.

Peres, J., & Nasello, A. G. (2007). Psychotherapy and neuroscience: Towards closer integration. *International Journal of Psychology,* 1–15.

Perry, S., Frances, A., Klar, H., et al. (1983). Selection criteria for individual dynamic psychotherapies. *Psychiatric Quarterly, 55,* 3–16.

Phillips, L. E. (1987). The ubiquitous decay curve: Delivery similarities in psychotherapy, medicine and addiction. *Professional Psychology: Research and Practice, 18,* 650–652.

Pietromonaco, P. R., & Feldman Barrett, L. (2000). The internal working models concept: What do we really know about the self in relation to others? *Review of General Psychology, 4,* 155–175.

Pincus, A. L., & Ansell, E. B. (2003). Interpersonal theory of personality. In T. Millon & M. Lerner (Eds.), *Handbook of psychology—Vol.5: Personality and social psychology* (pp. 209–229). New York, NY: Wiley.

Piper, W. E., Azim, H. F. A., Joyce, A. S., & McCallum, M. (1991). Transference interpretations, therapeutic alliance, and outcome in short-term individual psychotherapy. *Archives of General Psychiatry, 48,* 946–953.

Piper, W. E., Debbane, E. G., Bienvenu, J. P., & Garant, J. (1984). A comparative study of four forms of psychotherapy. *Journal of Consulting and Clinical Psychology, 52,* 268–279.

Piper, W. E., Ogrodniczuk, J. S., Joyce, A. S., McCallum, M., Rosie, J. S., O'Kelley, J. G., & Steinberg, P. I. (1999). Prediction of dropping out in time-limited, interpretive individual psychotherapy. *Psychotherapy: Theory, Research, Practice, Training, 36,* 114–122.

Poe, E. A. (1844/2000). The purloined letter. In S. Levine & S. F. Levine (Eds.), *Thirty-Two Stories* (pp. 256–271). Indianapolis, IN: Hackett.

Preston, J., Varzos, N., & Liebert, D. (1995). *Every session counts: Making the most of your brief therapy.* San Luis Obispo, CA: Impact.

Price, J., Hilsenroth, M., Callahan, K., Petretic-Jackson, P., & Bonge, D. (2004). A pilot study of psychodynamic psychotherapy for adult survivors of childhood sexual abuse. *Clinical Psychology and Psychotherapy, 11,* 378–391.

Quintana, S. M., & Meara, N. M. (1990). Internalization of the therapeutic relationship in short term psychotherapy. *Journal of Counseling Psychology, 37,* 123–130.

Rachman, A. W. (1988). Rule of empathy: Sandor Ferenczi's pioneering contribution to the empathic method in psychoanalysis. *Journal of the American Academy of Psychoanalysis, 16*, 1–27.

Rank, O. (1929/1936). *Will therapy* (J. Taft, Trans.). New York, NY: Knopf.

Rau, F. (1989, February). *Length and stay in therapy: Myths and reality.* Paper presented at the annual convention of the California State Psychological Association, San Francisco.

Rawson, P. (2005). *Handbook of short-term psychodynamic psychotherapy.* London, England: Karnac.

Reik, T. (1948). *Listening with the third ear.* New York, NY: Grove Press.

Ridley, C. R., & Kelly, S. M. (2007) Multicultural considerations in case formulation. In T. D. Eells (Ed.), *Handbook of psychotherapy case formulation* (pp. 33–64). New York, NY: Guilford Press.

Robertson, J. (1953). *A two-year-old goes to the hospital* [Film]. University Park, PA: Penn State Audio Visual Services.

Sadler, P., Woody, E., & Ethier, N. (in press). Complementarity in interpersonal relationships. In L. Horowitz & S. Strack (Eds.), *Handbook of interpersonal psychology.* New York, NY: Wiley.

Safran, J. D., & Muran, J. C. (1996). The resolution of ruptures in the therapeutic alliance. *Journal of Consulting and Clinical Psychology, 64*, 447–458.

Safran, J. D., & Muran, J. C. (2000). *Negotiating the therapeutic alliance: A relational treatment guide.* New York, NY: Guilford Press.

Safran, J. D., & Segal, Z. V. (1990). *Interpersonal process in cognitive therapy.* New York, NY: Basic Books.

Sampson, H., & Weiss, J. (1986). Testing hypotheses: The approach of the Mount Zion Psychotherapy Research Group. In L. S. Greenberg & N. M. Pinsof (Eds.), *The psychotherapeutic process: A research handbook* (pp. 591–613). New York, NY: Guilford Press.

Sanderson, W. C. (2002). Comment on Hansen et al.: Would the results be the same if patients were receiving an evidence-based treatment? Clinical *Psychology: Science and Practice, 9*, 350–352.

Sandler, J. (1976). Counter-transference and role-responsiveness. *International Review of Psychoanalysis, 3*, 43–47.

Schacht, T. E. (1991). Can psychotherapy education advance psychotherapy integration? *Journal of Psychotherapy Integration, 1*, 305–319.

Schacht, T. E., Binder, J. L, & Strupp, H. H. (1984). The dynamic focus. In H. H. Strupp & J. L. Binder (Eds.), *Psychotherapy in a new key* (pp. 65–109). New York, NY: Basic Books.

Schore, A. N. (1994). *Affect regulation and the organization of self*. Hillsdate, NJ: Erlbaum.

Schore, A. N. (2003a). *Affect regulation and the repair of the self*. New York, NY: Norton.

Schore, A. N. (2003b). Early relational trauma, disorganized attachment, and the development of a predisposition to violence. In M. F. Solomon, (Ed.), *Healing trauma: Attachment, mind, body, and brain*. New York, NY: Norton.

Schore, A. N. (2006, May/June). Right brain attachment dynamics: An essential mechanism of psychotherapy. *The California Psychologist, 6–8.*

Schore, A. N. (2009, August). *Paradigm shift: The right brain and the relational unconscious*. Presentation at the American Psychological Association Convention, Toronto, Ontario, Canada.

Seligman, M. (1995). The effectiveness of psychotherapy: The Consumer Reports study. *American Psychologist, 50,* 965–974.

Shapiro, D. A., Barkham., M., Rees, A., Hardy, G. E., Reynolds, S., & Startup, M. (1994). Effects of treatment duration and severity of depression on the effectiveness of cognitive–behavioral and psychodynamic–interpersonal psychotherapy. *Journal of Consulting and Clinical Psychology, 62,* 522–534.

Shapiro, D., Rees, A., Barkham, M., Hardy, G., Reynolds, S., & Startup, M. (1995). Effects of treatment duration and severity of depression on the maintenance of gains after cognitive–behavioral and psychodynamic–interpersonal psychotherapy. *Journal of Consulting and Clinical Psychology, 63,* 378–387.

Shaver, P. R., & Mikulincer, M. (2008). An overview of adult attachment theory. In J. H. Obegi & E. Berant (Eds.), *Attachment theory and research in clinical work with adults* (pp. 17–45). New York, NY: Guilford Press.

Siegel, D. J. (1999). *The developing mind: Toward a neurobiology of interpersonal experience*. New York, NY: Guilford Press.

Siegel, D. J. (2006). An interpersonal neurobiology approach to psychotherapy. *Psychiatric Annals, 36,* 248–256.

Siegel, D. J. (2007). *The mindful brain*. New York, NY: Norton.

Siegel, D. J., & Hartzell, M. (2003). *Parenting from the inside out: How a deeper self-understanding can help you raise children who thrive*. New York, NY: Tarcher/Putnam.

Sifneos, P. E. (1979/1987). *Short-term dynamic psychotherapy: Evaluation and technique.* New York, NY: Plenum.

Sledge, W. H., Moras, K., Hartley, D., & Levine, M. (1990). Effect of time-limited psychotherapy on patient dropout rates. *American Journal of Psychiatry, 147,* 1341–1347.

Spitz, R. (1947). Hospitalism: A follow-up report on investigation described in Volume 1, 1945. *The Psychoanalytic Study of the Child, 2,* 113–117.

Sterba, R. (1951). A case of brief psychotherapy by Sigmund Freud. *Psychoanalytic Review, 38,* 75–80.

Stern, D. N. (1985). *The interpersonal world of the infant.* New York, NY: Basic Books.

Stern, D. N. (2004). *The present moment: In psychotherapy and everyday life.* New York, NY: Norton.

Stern, D. N., & Process of Change Study Group. (1998). The process of therapeutic change involving implicit knowledge: Some implications of developmental observations for adult psychotherapy. *Infant Mental Health Journal, 19,* 300–308.

Stroufe, L.A., & Waters, E. (1977). Attachment as an organizational construct. *Child Development, 48,* 1184–1199.

Strupp, H. H. (1955a). An objective comparison of Rogerian and psychoanalytic techniques. *Journal of Consulting Psychology, 19,* 1–7.

Strupp, H. H. (1955b). The effect of the psychotherapist's personal analysis upon his techniques. *Journal of Consulting Psychology, 19,* 197–204.

Strupp, H. H. (1955c). Psychotherapeutic technique, professional affiliation, and experience level. *Journal of Consulting Psychology, 19,* 97–102.

Strupp, H. H. (1960). *Psychotherapists in action: Explorations of the therapist's contribution to the treatment process.* New York, NY: Grune & Stratton.

Strupp, H. H. (1980). Success and failure in time-limited psychotherapy: A systematic comparison of two cases (Comparison 1). *Archives of General Psychiatry, 37,* 595–603.

Strupp, H. H., & Binder, J. L. (1984). *Psychotherapy in a new key.* New York, NY: Basic Books.

Sue, S., Zane, N., & Young, K. (1994). Research on psychotherapy with culturally diverse populations. In A. E. Bergin & S. L. Garfield (Eds.), *Handbook of psychotherapy and behavior change* (4th ed., pp. 783–820). New York, NY: Wiley.

Sullivan, H. S. (1927). Affective experience in early schizophrenia. *American Journal of Psychiatry, 6,* 467–483.

Sullivan, H. S. (1953). *The interpersonal theory of psychiatry.* New York, NY: Norton.

Sullivan, H. S. (1954). *The psychiatric interview*. New York, NY: Norton.

Swift, J. K., Callahan, J., & Levine, J. C. (2009). Using clinically significant change to identify premature termination. *Psychotherapy: Theory, Research, Practice, Training, 46*, 328–335.

Taft, J. (1958). *Otto Rank*. New York, NY: Julian Press.

Talley, P. F., Strupp, H. H., & Butler, S. F. (Eds.). (1994). *Psychotherapy, research, and practice*. New York, NY: Basic Books.

Thackrey, M., Butler, S. F., & Strupp, H. H. (1993). The Capacity for Dynamic Process Scale (CDPS). In M. L. Canfield & J. E. Canfield (Eds.), *A collection of psychological scales* (pp. 191–210). New York, NY: Basic Books.

Tomkins, S. (1963). *Affect, imagery and consciousness: The negative affects (Vol 1)*. New York, NY: Springer.

Travis, L. A., Binder, J. L., Bliwise, N. G., & Horne-Moyer, H. L. (2001). Changes in clients' attachment styles over the course of time-limited dynamic psychotherapy. *Psychotherapy, 38*, 149–159.

Tronick, E. Z. (1989). Emotions and emotional communication in infants. *American Psychologist, 44*, 112–119.

Tronick, E. Z., Als, H., Adamson, L., Wise, S., & Brazelton, T. B. (1978). The infant's response to entrapment between contradictory messages in face-to-face interaction. *Journal of the American Academy of Child Psychiatry, 17*, 1–13.

Ursano, R. J., & Hales, R. E. (1986). A review of brief individual psychotherapies. *American Journal of Psychiatry, 143*, 1507–1517.

Van der Kolk, B. A., McFarlane, A., & Weisath, L. (1996). Traumatic stress. New York, NY: Guilford Press.

von Bertalanffy, L. (1969). *General systems theory* (Rev. ed.). New York, NY: Braziller.

Wachtel, P. L. (1993). *Therapeutic communication*. New York, NY: Guilford Press.

Wachtel, P. L. (2008). *Relational theory and the practice of psychotherapy*. New York, NY: Guilford Press.

Walter, B. (1940). *Theme and variation*. New York, NY: Knopf.

Weiss, J. (1993). *How psychotherapy works*. New York, NY: Guilford.

Weiss, J., Sampson, H., & Mount Zion Psychotherapy Research Group. (1986). *The psychoanalytic process: Theory, clinical observations, and empirical research*. New York, NY: Guilford Press.

Welfel, E. R. (2004). The ethical challenges of brief therapy. In D. P. Chapman (Ed.), *Core processes in brief psychodynamic psychotherapy* (pp. 343–359). Mahwah, NJ: Erlbaum.

Westen, D., Novotny, C. M., & Thompson-Brenner, H. (2004). The empirical status of empirically supported psychotherapies. *Psychological Bulletin, 130,* 631–663.

Whelton, W. J. (2004). Emotional process in psychotherapy: Evidence across therapeutic modalities. *Clinical Psychology and Psychotherapy, 111,* 89–106.

White, M., & Epston, D. (1990). *Literate means to therapeutic ends.* Adelaide, Australia: Dulwich Centre.

Wierzbicki, M., & Pekarik, G. (1993). A meta-analysis of psychotherapy dropout. *Professional Psychology: Research and Practice, 24,* 190–195.

Wiggins, J. S. (1979). A psychological taxonomy of trait-descriptive terms: The interpersonal domain. *Journal of Personality and Social Psychology, 37,* 395–412.

Wilkinson, S. M., & Gabbard, G. O. (1993). Therapeutic self-disclosure with borderline patients. *Journal of Psychotherapy Practice and Research, 2,* 282–295.

Wolf, E. (1986). Discrepancies between analysand and analyst in experiencing the analysis. In A. Goldberg (Ed.), *Progress in self psychology II.* New York, NY: Guilford Press.

Wolstein, B. (1983). The pluralism of perspectives on counter-transference. *Contemporary Psychoanalysis, 19,* 506–521.

Yalom, I. D. (1995). *The theory and practice of group psychotherapy* (4th ed.). New York, NY: Basic Books.

# Index

# About the Author

**Hanna Levenson, PhD,** has been specializing in the area of brief psychotherapy as a clinician, teacher/trainer, and researcher for 30 years. She is the author of more than 75 papers and two books, the *Concise Guide to Brief Dynamic and Interpersonal Psychotherapy* (2002) and *Time-Limited Dynamic Psychotherapy: A Guide to Clinical Practice* (1995), which was selected by the Behavioral Science Book Service as a "book-of-the-month." She also has three professional videos, *Making Every Session Count* (1999), *Time-Limited Dynamic Psychotherapy* (2008), and *Brief Dynamic Therapy Over Time* (2009).

In 2000, she founded the Levenson Institute for Training, a center where mental health practitioners can receive in-depth training and certification in integrative, focused therapy. Dr. Levenson is a professor of psychology at the Wright Institute in Berkeley and director of the Brief Psychotherapy Program at California Pacific Medical Center in San Francisco. For 20 years, she was clinical professor at the Department of Psychiatry, University of California School of Medicine and director of the Brief Psychotherapy Program at the San Francisco VA Medical Center.

Dr. Levenson's professional career reflects a 30-year dialectic between intrapsychic and relational perspectives, insight and experiential learning, and clinical practice and scientific inquiry. Originally trained in personality theory and social psychology at Claremont University, she later retrained in clinical psychology at the University of Florida, Coral Gables, then interned at Langley Porter Institute (University of California, San Francisco, School of Medicine) in 1976.

In addition to her teaching and writing, she maintains a private practice in San Francisco and Oakland, California, and is also a certified therapist and supervisor in emotionally focused couples therapy.

Dr. Levenson is a member of the American Psychological Association and a Fellow of Division 29 (Psychotherapy), the California Psychological Association, the Society for Psychotherapy Research, the Society for the Exploration of Psychotherapy Integration, and the International Centre for Excellence in Emotionally Focused Therapy.